The Art of Christian Caring

The Art of Christian Caring

Marcus D. Bryant

The Bethany Press
St. Louis, Missouri

Address: The Bethany Press, Box 179, St. Louis, MO 63166.

Photographs by Bob Taylor.

Library of Congress Cataloging in Publication Data

Bryant, Marcus David.
The art of Christian caring.

1. Visitations (Church work) I. Title.
BV4320.B79 253 78-20791
ISBN 0-8272-0015-3

Distributed in Canada by The G. R. Welch Company, Ltd., Toronto, Ontario, Canada

Printed in the United States of America

Contents

To my wife, Virginia, and to our children, Barbara and Steven, through whom caring continues to be a way of living.

Acknowledgements

I wish to express gratitude to three persons who have helped me significantly in this writing project. My wife, Virginia, read the manuscript for style and expression, as well as for error. The manuscript was typed in its entirety by Mrs. Rebecca McNitt, and the detailed outline for the book was reviewed by my colleague at Brite Divinity School, Dr. Charles F. Kemp. Each of these persons was a source of special encouragement.

Preface

Christian persons in many churches show increasing interest in carrying out personal ministries. The history of the church shows that this activity is cyclical. Recent practices in American churches have been to invest the pastor almost entirely with pastoral care, with good reason. The pastor has been more adequately educated and trained to carry out specialized tasks of pastoral care. As the pastor became more fully trained, neither the pastor nor the church members believed lay persons should participate in the ministry of pastoral care. In some respects this remains true, particularly in pastoral counseling, which is one important part of pastoral care.

However, all people need to continue carrying out some aspects of Christian caring. Caring for one another, especially in times of special need, is at the heart of Christian living. Some ways of activating this caring are more effective and responsible than others. This book is an attempt to highlight these better ways, especially for persons in special need. Friendships among active members of the churches are inspiring and strengthening. There are others among us who miss this strength and inspiration, often because the active persons hesitate, for lack of confidence and information, to express their care.

The need for caring among Christian persons is great; the opportunities for caring are limitless. The intent of this book is to provide encouragement and guidelines for the art of Christian caring.

Greater love has no man than this, that a man lay down his life for his friends.

John 15:13

Civilization is, at least in part, a form of crystallized love. And it is time now that we begin to examine the case for caring and for love.

Man cares because it is his nature to care. Man survives because he cares and is cared for.

Willard Gaylin

1

The Caring Relationship

Human beings care for other persons. Caring is at the heart of the human relationship. In a time when it seems popular to present persons as blasé, cool, and not needing involvement with others, it is important to recover our sense of belonging. For the Christian, the very source of life itself is love—God is love. Conception, birth, and growth are ordered processes designed to bring into the world, and to nurture, caring persons. Willard Gaylin writes, "If there is one fact founded in his biology, essential to his survival and uniquely his own, it is that *Homo sapiens* is supremely a loving animal and a caring one."[1]

The Christian has always believed this. The harsh experiences of rejection, care-less-ness, and human violence shake our trust. As a result, we withdraw in uncertainty and fear, limiting our caring relationships with others. This withdrawal can become the beginning of alienation from others, from God, and from ourselves.

Two news stories reported on television, one following the other, are examples. In the first account, a sixteen-year-old girl was on trial for the murder of her mother and the attempted murder of her father. In the second, a mother was accused of beating her nine-

1. *Caring*. Alfred A. Knopf, 1976, p. 10.

year-old daughter and leaving her to drown in a lake. We recoil from such events in confusion and fear. Spoken or unspoken, the questions are, "How could any parent treat a child that way?" and "What would make a teenager kill both parents?" We know this isn't the way life is supposed to be, and so the questions plague us. The violent acts erase all else from our minds. Yet the violent ones also were cared for and loved, and their desperate need still is to be loved and cared for. Violence between persons obscures our understanding that human beings care because it is their nature to care.

Nurtured Into Life

All of us have been nurtured into life. For a year following birth, the human infant's development, so dramatically begun in the mother's womb, is just being completed. The newborn baby's life fully depends upon the care of others. Our own capacity to care—to love—found its force and direction in those days of life's beginning. The give-and-take between infant and parent becomes the seed for growth into all life's caring relationships.

As one grows, the nurturance continues, and the person expands in the ability to receive and to give—to care. From the first breath of life, we respond to love and to care—we learn that our lives depend upon it and it is natural to give love and care in response. We love because love has nurtured us. We care because we have first been cared for. Learning that we are loved and that we can love in return takes place in the interaction between infant and parent. We have not learned to love in isolation, and if we are to give love, there must be someone there to receive it and to acknowledge it.

The preoccupation of many persons is with seeking love, not giving it. A pastoral counselor was counseling with Mrs. Johnson, a forty-three-year-old woman who was recovering from her second divorce when she told him she thought she had found her third husband.

"Do you love him?" the counselor asked.

"I don't know. How do you know when you love someone?"

"When you married your first husband, did you love him?" the counselor asked.

Mrs. Johnson's response was, "I did when I married him, but it didn't take long for me to know he didn't love me!"

As she continued in counseling, Mrs. Johnson came to understand her inability to trust others, and her limited ability to give love. Her motivation in marriage was to get love, but she was unable to give it freely. She discovered this to be true in all her relationships.

Most persons are like Mrs. Johnson in one respect. We depend upon nurturance into life long after we have left infancy. But just as we depend upon the care of others, particularly those close to us, so do they depend upon our caring for them—our nurturance of them. Love comes alive as the caring ones move toward one another.

Loving Self and Neighbor

Mrs. Johnson had grown up in family relationships which made it difficult for her to love herself. The reassurance that she was lovable became her test of the marriage relationship. Constantly seeking this reassurance, she could not freely give love to someone else.

We not only learn to love others because others have loved us, but we learn to love *ourselves* because others have first loved us! Jesus understood this and recognized the importance of a healthy self-love when he taught that a person is to love one's neighbor *as oneself*. This does not mean that we are to be self-centered or selfish. Rather, it means that in accepting the love and care of others, we have come to know ourselves as being lovable. We have gained a trust and a confidence in ourselves as being worthy of another person's caring for us.

Being created in the image of God is to be created in the image of love. In the experiences of life where we are loved and cared for, we learn we are lovable and gain the desire and the means to care for others and to love them.

Clark Moustakas tells of Elizabeth and her family. Elizabeth was born a third child, and before they left the hospital, her parents learned that a malformed vertebra would not allow her to live. The baby was not expected to leave the hospital, but she did, and she lived several months longer with her family. Her parents and brothers loved her and carefully cared for her, and she responded to their love. She lived longer than the physicians had thought possible, but finally she had to give up her life.

> Elizabeth, by being, seemed to release the love of all the persons who knew her and this releasing of love seemed to spread throughout her family . . . to the neighbors, to friends, to persons in other communities and other states.[2]

The family felt love returned from their baby, and their love enabled her to grow in the exchange. Though Elizabeth's life was cut short, Elizabeth's parents and brothers saw the seeds of love and care begin to sprout and grow in her. That love and care was nurtured in the family and it spread all around. In coming to know ourselves as being lovable and in caring for others, we discover the power in loving our neighbors as we love ourselves.

Love in Friendships

Friendship is love. C. S. Lewis has helped us to distinguish among four types of love: affection, friendship, eros, and charity.[3] There is both "need love" and "gift love" in each of us and while affection is a "need love," it is with friendship that we begin to

---

2. *Loneliness*. Prentice-Hall, 1961, p. 11.
3. *The Four Loves*. Harcourt Brace & Co., 1960.

experience "gift love" in significant ways. Love that is friendship seems to be experienced less and less. As Lewis points out, "Without Eros none of us would have been begotten and without Affection none of us would have been reared; but we can live and breed without Friendship." Such a life, while Lewis deems it possible, would indeed be a barren life, hardly worth living. Indeed, those suffering persons who come to believe their only option is to end their own lives usually have not felt the full force of love that is friendship.

There are several important characteristics of friendship. In reading from the thirteenth chapter of Paul's first letter to the church at Corinth, one is struck by the description as that belonging to true friendship. Some of these are only another way of presenting them.

1. Friendship is marked by the person's discovery of a "kindred soul." This usually arises out of a companionship when two people realize they perceive and value things in similar ways. The discovery that someone else, so different from me, can see and feel as I do—this discovery belongs to friendship.

2. Friendship knows no sexual distinction. A man's close friend might be a man or woman and vice versa. Of course, love that is friendship can become love that is eros, or sexual love. We encourage youth to seek true friendship with a potential mate, before marriage. Hopefully, love that is friendship will continue in married love.

3. Friendship is not limited in number. Friendship is personal but not exclusive. Two friends are happily joined by a third and a fourth, as long as all have the attributes of true friends. When the "open-ness" between two friends becomes the "closed-ness" toward other friendships, love is warped and changed.

4. Friendship knows no class or social barrier. While many of us relate most easily with persons somewhat like ourselves in background, education, religion, occupation, vocation, etc., these are not

essential for friendship. Persons from differing social classes can and do find common identifications in forming friendships.

5. Friendship is nonpossessive. One friend does not control, manage, or manipulate another. Friendship is being side-by-side, free to move away and free to move back. Its strength and essence is in the mutually respected integrity of the other.

6. Friendship does not pry or probe. Friends share personal information out of the wish to do so, not from necessity. This sharing is an offering of the self—the giving of one person to the other. One friend hears such an offering without needing to change, judge, or argue, but to respond honestly with one's own self.

7. Friendship is loyal. A true friend is sometimes regarded as one whom "I can count on, no matter what." Yet, friendship is more than "help" in an emergency. Helping in time of special need is more true for love as affection, than love as friendship. The loyalty of friends is not measured and one good deed is not traded off against another. Good deeds are done, of course, but are not ends themselves in friendship.

8. Friendship engenders humility. A friend feels fortunate to be valued, accepted, and cared for as a person. This results in a growing humility. "How lucky I am to be your friend" is often the reaction.

Friendship includes these characteristics and more. With all of them love is there, for friendship is love. Jesus talked with his disciples about love and being friends. He spoke of loving the disciples as the Father had loved him. Then he told them that the greatest love a person can have is to lay down one's life for friends, and that whereas he had earlier called them servants, now he calls them friends. Here Jesus makes an interesting distinction between servant and friend. The servant does not know what his master does, but the friends know what there is to know of importance between them, "for all that I have heard from my Father I have made known to you" (John 15:15).

Risk and Courage in Friendship

Any significant human relationship bears its risk. So it is with friendship. The exchanges between persons carry with them the risk of self-disclosure. Risking is acting in spite of a possible painful outcome as well as a possible joyful one. What are the risks of self-disclosure? Whatever they are, they add up to the risk of being rejected by the other person.

In offering myself to another, I risk his or her indifference. Indifference is a form of rejection. Each of us bears rejection in different ways. If I have not come to love myself, or to see myself as being lovable, indifference from another is a cruel blow. On the other hand, if I have come to know myself as being lovable, as being worthy of love from another, I can tolerate some indifference. Still, for all of us, to disclose anything of importance to another is to run the risk of indifference in the other person.

Another risk of self-disclosure is that I will be judged harshly or criticized. Criticism is always painful. This is especially true when I have opened myself to another person in trust, in order to give myself, in order to care. If I offer myself and my offering is met with judgment and criticism, my tendency is to withdraw in my hurt.

In my self-disclosure, I also risk not being taken seriously. Again, this is a form of rejection, and the temptation is to retreat into the closed bantering which the other person obviously prefers to a growing relationship.

But the risks of self-disclosure are necessary and by no means is rejection the only outcome. The risks are run to enable one person to reach out to another, and for the other person to respond. And many do. We run the risk in order to live together, to grow together, and to care for one another. Often, the risk of being rejected never materializes, and the caring relationship is born, or enhanced. The risk is run not only for one person, but for two or three, or more. This is always true in human relationships.

Dr. Sidney Jourard has done exhaustive studies of self-disclosure and writes, "We are learning that sharing one's authentic experiencing with another has important effects upon both the discloser and the listener."[4] Sharing with others enables us to learn more about ourselves. This is as important as it is to listen to another person. Counselors who listen to others also find their counselors with whom they can share from the depths of their own lives.

Reaching out always requires courage. Marc Oraison demonstrates that to reach out to form a new relationship is to put one in conflict. He writes, "If one fails to recognize that it is the conflict as such that establishes the relationship, since that is in fact what happens, the relationship is illusory, and when one is finally forced to face the truth, it can be irreparably destroyed."[5] The conflict is in the coming together of two distinct and different individuals, seeking to communicate and to relate. It is this element of conflict which keeps us, at times, from making the effort to reach out to another person.

The risk of reaching out, of self-disclosure, the conflict of forming and developing relationships is necessary. It is necessary because of our need for each other and to exercise our natural being of loving and caring.

Giving to Others

Caring persons know the joy of giving. I have spoken of the love of friendship as gift-love. Generally, there are two ways of giving: giving things and giving self. Both are important. In many instances, the gifts we buy or create are symbolic expressions of something of ourselves. When I receive such a gift, it has lasting and special meaning for me. However, the direct giving of self, such as the sharing of positive

4. *The Transparent Self*. D. Van Nostrand, 2nd ed., 1971, p. 60.
5. *Being Together*. Image Books, 1971, p. 94.

feelings toward another person, is the more crucial kind of giving in human relationships.

Some persons find it very difficult to share their inner thoughts and feelings with others. Many persons have difficulty knowing what their feelings are and depend upon ideas, attitudes, and events in communicating with others. Such persons more naturally give things to express themselves. There are persons, for example, who work hard to earn money in order to buy gifts for their spouses. Sometimes the spouse mistakes the gift for bribery because the marriage partner has difficulty putting his or her love feelings in words. In this case, the dollars earned from hard work become the means for expressing love. Someone has called them "love dollars."

Growth in the ability to give self directly to other persons is essential both for the sake of the giver and the receiver. In order to do this, one must be aware of one's own feelings, learning to express them in ways that are helpful to self and to others. David Viscott writes, "Our feelings are our sixth sense, the sense that interprets, arranges, directs, and summarizes the other five."[6] In order to give of myself, to share my positive feelings toward others, I must grow in my awareness of feelings and allow them expression in positive ways.

There are many ways that you can share yourself with others. Each person finds the ways that are most comfortable for him or her. Here are four ways of giving self in the art of caring. They may suggest others to you.

1. The expression of your loving concern. This expression can take many forms, but *verbal* expression is basic. Usually, caring persons are aware of loving concerns that go unexpressed. When they are not directly communicated to the other person, both are denied the resulting joy and strength. Like others, you may not know what to say or how to say it. Speak of your concern in ways most natural for you. Upon the death of a parent, a friend said to a bereaved woman, "I

6. *The Language of Feelings*. Arbor House, 1976, p. 11.

just heard of your father's death and I want you to know of my love for you, especially now." No more was needed. Words and manner communicated fully the loving concern.

2. Your presence. Your physical presence with a friend is often the most significant way of sharing yourself. In times of crisis or during long periods of waiting, the presence of a concerned friend is strengthening. On other occasions, a brief visit in the home or at work may be the best way of giving yourself. Your presence is symbolic of the genuine compassion you feel and is understood as such by your friend. In many instances few words are exchanged. Presence is enough.

Ron Wilson had been waiting an hour outside surgery while his wife was undergoing an open-heart operation. He was anxious and time moved very slowly. Then Jim Horton came in to sit with Ron. They visited awhile. Then Jim realized that Ron really didn't feel like carrying on a conversation, so they sat together and waited. Later, Ron told Jim, "Your staying with me got me through those difficult hours." The presence of a caring person can be a priceless gift.

3. Another way of giving yourself is the offering of your skills or talent. Many of us have been recipients of this kind of giving. I remember my grandfather going to the farm of a sick neighbor to do the milking and feeding the livestock every morning and evening for days, until the neighbor could do his own work once more. More is at stake here than just "helping out." It is the willingness, the desire, even the *need* to use one's strength and abilities for the sake of a friend which is important. A friend donating a pint of blood when you need it carries a double meaning: the healing agent of the blood, and knowing your friend gives it for *you*.

4. Giving your time is a way of giving yourself. While the use of time is involved in the three other ways discussed here, the use of time deserves mention in itself. When you show that you gladly *choose* to use time to express your friendship, most persons

accept it gratefully. Time is precious, and so are friends. Building and maintaining relationships involve giving time.

Our relationships are enriched by the unique and genuine ways we find to express our friendship—to give ourselves to others. The art of Christian caring centers in the ways we give ourselves to others.

Receiving from Others

There is an art to receiving as well as giving. It has been referred to as the "grace" of receiving. When you give a gift, you are pleased when it is received graciously. Many persons find this gracious receiving difficult to do. It is not unusual for generous and loving persons to give to others, but find it difficult to receive a gift. Also, there are persons who can receive articles as gifts, but find themselves embarrassed in accepting a loving gesture, a caring service.

Many hundreds of persons who have participated in growth groups have discovered their inability to receive graciously. Early in my experience of sharing in such groups, I was confronted by my fellow group members when I ignored a direct compliment. They helped me to become aware of how I felt when complimented and why I was reluctant to acknowledge the compliment and to respond to it. It was a valuable lesson to learn.

Ministers and others who have a commitment to serving other persons often find receiving care more difficult than giving. For example, ministers who are used to comforting others are thrown off balance when ill and being comforted by their friends or fellow ministers. One minister friend, recuperating in the hospital, commented, "I need to get out of this bed—I have so many sick and shut-in people to call on!" He really wasn't able to give attention to the care I had brought to share with him. He was an excellent care "giver," but a poor care "receiver."

There are several attitudes and feelings which inhibit persons from receiving graciously. Among the most common are these.

1. "I shouldn't have to depend upon someone else, so I don't want to acknowledge how good it feels to receive a gift!" While the logic of this is questionable, there is a definite connection. Many of us have learned that we should never receive a gift without "paying back." To receive a gift then is to become "beholden" and to be in debt to the person. This is a form of dependency that many people want to avoid. If this is the way I feel, I may let a compliment slide by without acknowledging it. Thus a gift from my friend is not accepted.

2. "I don't want to show any self-centeredness, so I will not let a gift become so important to me." There is an attitude that seems to say, "to show too much delight in receiving means I like to get rather than to give." This one is a hazard for Christian persons! Our religion encourages us, rightly so, to be concerned about others first. Unfortunately, we develop guilt feelings because we have self-interests. Since we need the love and care of others, we enjoy receiving gifts. It is important then to let our joy be expressed to receive a gift for what it is and to respond with gratitude.

3. Perhaps not as common as the first two, but one which many persons experience is the attitude, "I can't believe that someone would think that I am as good as they tell me I am, so I won't play their game and give their compliment (gift) much attention." Behind such an attitude is personal insecurity. If I am insecure, since I do not feel worthy of such a gift (compliment), the other person *really* couldn't either, so I can't trust his or her sincerity. This attitude can be a problem in another way. Oftentimes, a person mistakes this for humility (either on the part of the giver or the receiver, or both). Obviously, not feeling secure in my own worth is not the same as having humility. I need to learn to accept my worth in the sight of God, in relationship with other

persons, and then I can find positive ways of exercising humility.

4. There is another attitude that inhibits a person's receiving graciously: "Strong people give, weak ones receive." This is a mistaken attitude that seems to arise from observing the helpless newborn infant and from our own childhood experiences. The mistake here is to assume the infant cannot give; an infant can, and does give. The love and the response the infant gives to caring parents, we have already recognized, demonstrate the giving power of the helpless infant. Children of all ages also give and show their strength in various ways while being taken care of. Giving does not necessarily equal strength; receiving does not equal weakness.

Our Christian concern for giving can blind us to the art of receiving. We are created with amazing powers of receptivity, and the Scriptures reflect their crucial role in our relationship with God and one another. Proverbs 20:12 is a clear example: "The hearing ear, and the seeing eye, the Lord hath made them both." When Jesus was speaking with the crowds and his disciples in parables and the disciples asked him why, he responded, "This is why I speak to them in parables, because seeing they do not see, and hearing they do not hear, nor do they understand. . . . But blessed are your eyes, for they see, and your ears, for they hear" (Matt. 13:13, 16). Jesus used the trust and receptivity of the little children as models for adults. Our openness to the gifts of others, our freedom to accept them joyfully, without guilt or apology, can be a mark of that trust and receptivity.

As we express care and concern for others, and we experience hesitancy on their part, we can understand and accept their struggle without being hurt or deterred by it. We continue to exercise our caring and our loving. Our acceptance of them in their struggle to receive can become the means whereby they learn the art and the joy of receiving.

The Caring Community

The church is a caring community. It is so by nature and by practice. Believers speak of the church as the "body of Christ in the world." Members refer to the church as the "fellowship of faith" and talk of their church "family" or church "friends." This community is the context of Christian caring. Daniel Day Williams, in a discussion of the church and the healing of the human spirit, pursued several lines in defining the church, then concluded by saying, "It is the true Christian community holding out hope for the nurture and health of spirit of those within it when it is animated by the spirit of acceptance, of reconciliation, and of service."[7]

There are several truths to be considered as we think of the church as a caring community. First, the church is imperfect. We are human—imperfect and sinning. This does not change the truth that the church is a "fellowship of the saints." A saint is a forgiven sinner. Christians have always believed the church to be where the Spirit of God—the Holy Spirit—dwells. It is this spirit of love, acceptance, and forgiveness that has come to be real in the lives of those who work and who worship there. It is this very spirit that not only reveals our imperfection but points us beyond sin to hope found in forgiveness and loving. Forgiveness and love are of God but they are also human characteristics, and it is in the church that we find the hope that love and forgiveness can be manifested in us.

Second, the church is where loved and forgiven persons pursue a new life together. This also is a mark of the presence of God's spirit. This new life can best be understood in terms of a new *relationship*. The new relationship shows itself in a number of ways. There is trust, rather than fear or suspicion among the people. This trust leads to a spirit of general optimism, a

---

7. *The Minister and the Care of Souls*. Harper & Row, 1961, p. 146.

positive rather than a negative outlook. There is also acceptance of other persons as they are, rather than a judgment upon them. We seem to struggle much more in accepting ourselves and others as we are, than God ever has!

This new life or relationship also shows itself in the spirit of loving reconciliation. The interaction of human beings inevitably leads to breakdowns, feelings of anger and resentment, and rejection and hurt. New life together—or a new relationship does not mean none of this can exist in the church. Rather, it means that new ways of working out the trouble are possible. The redeemed are not perfect; rather they are redeemed from their otherwise self-destructive ways in the breakdown of human relationships. This is why the phrase "fellowship of reconciliation" has special meaning for the Christian. Reconciliation is a manifestation of the Spirit of God. It is always a mark of the *caring* community.

A third truth to be considered about the church as a caring community is that it is a *continuing* life in the spirit of love. More is involved in this continuance than worship or loving interaction among the members; it is in the giving of Christian *service*. Service is at the heart of a caring community. It has always been at the heart of the Christian church. At this point, we can see how the church is a caring community not only by its nature, but also in practice. Without the *practice* of love, the *nature* of love becomes meaningless for human beings. God as love becomes more real for us when we see it in the person of Jesus, the Christ. Christian service is not measurable; one can never get "caught up" in doing Christian service in the sense of completing it. This is because it has to do with our life and our relationships. As long as we are redeemed by God's love, we practice love, we render service.

While the context of Christian caring is the church, those in this continuing new relationship reach out to those beyond the fellowship. This is the nature of Christian love. This is the practice of Christian love. In a sense, Christian service is being with those who love you and those who do not love you. Christians have learned that there is no reward in loving only those who love them. We also have learned that there is but one true test of the existence of God's loving spirit among his people—the fruits of the Spirit. In other words, what is the outcome of my being loved and forgiven by God? My response is with my whole self—in terms of who I am, in the kind of relationships I have with others, and in service to others.

Christian caring is a response we make to God's love and forgiveness. Our response takes the form of being Christian through caring actions.

Teach me half the gladness
  That thy brain must know,
Such harmonious madness
  From my lips would flow
The world should listen then—as I am listening now!

Percy Bysshe Shelley

Then the eyes of those who see will
  not be closed,
and the ears of those who will hear
  will hearken.

Isaiah 32:3

2

Caring Through Listening

Listening is an art which can be learned and developed. Listening involves the interplay between two persons. We *listen* to another person in order to *hear;* we *hear* for the purpose of *understanding* and we seek to *understand* so we can accept this person. Earl Kiole writes, "Listening to one another and sharing our lives become means by which we nourish a sense of community in relationships and nourish also our freedom and individuality."[8] So listening is essential for the sake of the listener as well as the speaker. Caring is nurtured through listening. Listening engenders feelings of worth in the listener as well as in the speaker. It enables one to distinguish self from others and at the same time to value others more. Listening is a primary way we are affirmed as loving and caring persons.

As in many of our endeavors, most of us fail to listen at times. At such times, we miss the import of what the other person wants to express. Even when we think we are listening, we are dismayed at our failure to hear. Failing to hear the intended message of the

8. *Listening As a Way of Becoming*. Word Books, 1977, p. 22.

other person, we cannot understand, then have difficulty in accepting him or her.

What It Means to Listen

A dictionary definition of the word *listen* is to apply oneself to hearing something. Notice the active language: to "apply" oneself. Listening is active, not passive as one might suppose. I must apply myself to listening, as I must in realizing other accomplishments. It requires a fully conscious and thinking person.

To listen well, I must have an interest in the person who is speaking. My interest will be couched in my desire for the well-being of the person to whom I am listening. Therefore, my interest is not derived from curiosity to know what another person thinks and feels, or from the need to gossip. Rather, my interest is in taking responsibility to establish and nurture a caring relationship with the other person. Listening which becomes healing presence is born out of my interest in the person for his or her own sake, and my relationship with him or her.

Listening attentively encourages the other person to do the talking. There is a tendency for caring persons to believe they must talk in order to support or to comfort others. While some talking is necessary, a caring relationship involves the willingness and the ability to keep silent at appropriate times. Attentive listening enables a person to put frustrations and problems into words, and to begin to find directions and answers. The object in listening is not to hear a problem in order to offer a solution; rather, it is to hear a *person* so that the person may find clarity and self-direction.

As you listen carefully to another person, you find yourself listening to emotions as well as to words. Many times the person speaking has not fully realized his or her true feelings and the listener enables the discovery to take place.

Bill's voice grew louder and louder as he described his teacher. As Bill paused, red in the face and waving a clenched fist, Bill's father said, "You are really angry at your teacher." Bill yelled, "But I am *not* angry at the teacher!" Following a short silence, he said quietly, "I didn't realize how mad I was."

Other emotions emerge through and behind words as persons share important relationships and events. A careful listener will hear sadness and grief lurking behind a smiling face; will sense fear when listening to a person speak of a loved one. The one who speaks begins to sense the same things as they are listened to attentively. In many instances, the listener will need to say something such as, "You seem to be afraid," or "You seem sad to me." Often, the listener will need to say nothing, and the speaker gradually gains insight into his or her true feelings.

So listening utilizes all the senses, not just the ears. I listen with my eyes and my sensitivities to others' emotions. Theodor Reik speaks of this as "listening with the third ear."[9] It involves listening not only to the words that are spoken but to the way the words are used, the pitch of the voice and the rate of speech. It involves seeing the facial expression of the person speaking and observing the use of the body. "Body language" is central in communication, and as I listen to another person, this language becomes meaningful.

I also use body language as I listen. For example, if I am not truly attentive, I will reveal this in my body language. On one occasion, the person listening to me kept looking at something over my shoulder. I could not avoid turning around to see what he was looking at. There was nothing there; he just didn't look at me while I was speaking and I knew he wasn't listening carefully.

All about us there are persons who yearn to be listened to. They are members of our families, of our churches and schools, in factories and businesses. The need to listen and to be listened to arises out of our

---

9. *Listening with the Third Ear*. Grove Press, 1948.

need for each other, for companionship, friendship, for a continuing sense of worth. When someone says to you, "I want to talk with you, will you listen?" you have been paid a high compliment.

What It Means to Hear

We listen in order to hear each other. Two dictionary meanings are helpful. One meaning of "to hear" is to perceive (sound) by the ear. The other meaning is to learn by the speech of others. Both meanings are important in a caring relationship. We will not hear if we cannot perceive the sound. On the other hand, we may perceive the sound and not truly hear. In hearing, we also learn by the speech of others. To hear is to perceive meanings. Words are the symbols whereby we convey meanings to each other. We use a dictionary to use words precisely and consistently. At times, we have a problem in selecting the right words as symbols for the ideas, attitudes, feelings, and events which we wish to convey to each other. Most of us have felt the frustration in not finding the words to share a very important feeling or event. But when we find words which match what we feel, we convey what we intend. We are heard from when our listeners gain that same feeling and idea.

Words are not always necessary to convey meaning. Peter stood by Betty's bedside holding his wife's hand, looking into her eyes and seeing there the deep pain. Betty did not speak, but Peter said softly, "I hear you, honey!" Full communication had taken place, in this case without the need for words. Peter was looking, listening, and feeling—he heard.

When we truly hear, we often make use of images or pictures. This is what it means to become part of another person's world. This experience is part of every culture because it is central to human relationships. The American Indian refers to it as "walking in your brother's moccasins." The emotional result is to have empathy for another person. This is not possible until you are able to *hear* others, to perceive, to learn from them when you are listening.

It is not unusual for us to listen reasonably well to another person and yet have difficulty in truly *hearing* or getting the message. Most families experience one or another exclaiming, "But you have not heard me!" You may have been charged with that offense and thought you were listening quite well. There are numerous barriers both within and outside us that preclude hearing others. Some of the most important barriers to hearing are these.

1. Listening judgmentally. In growing up, we have learned the importance of "good and bad," "right and wrong." In fact, we learned very early that to be "wrong" was equal to being "bad" and to be "right" was to be "good." As adults, we are surprised at how early an age a child makes moral judgments, against self as well as others. From an early age, we practice listening to others in order to distinguish "error" or "untruth" or "un-goodness" in the other person. This is seen in couples whose marriage relationships are strained. Both partners of a couple may begin the counseling process believing the counselor will help them discover which one is "right" and which one is "wrong." They want to make the marriage counselor a judge who will listen judgmentally, just as they have been listening to each other in judgment. They discover how unhelpful this is when the counselor attempts to do that. As they learn that hearing judgmentally destroys their love, and they begin to listen to each other, and to *hear,* they learn being "right" is not the object: it is to hear, understand, and accept each other in love.

The goal is to listen, not with judgment but with understanding. Otherwise, it is difficult to hear what the other person is trying to say. As a listener, a check on yourself is to realize what you are thinking of your friend as you listen. You may expect to disagree with your friend on many things. For example, your friend may say, "I really don't like Jimmy, he is so unfriendly." You may be thinking to yourself how friendly you find Jimmy to be and really want to say so. It is better to try to hear your friend struggle aloud concerning this relationship which is unsatisfactory. Then, you may say something like, "you really find it difficult to be a friend with Jimmy." Your friend will more likely hear this response as a signal that you are listening and *hearing*.

2. A second barrier to hearing may be your own inner struggles. This is potentially true for every person —every listener. We bring to all our relationships our inner selves, and they are not always at ease. Our inner selves are often in conflict and anxious. When I am most anxious about my own life and therefore struggling within, I am not a good listener and may not be able to hear what you are saying. My need at this time is to seek someone who can listen to me and hear me.

George had joined a growth group eagerly but with no intention to reveal too much of himself. He discovered as he sat back offering little of himself that he began to feel left out and resentful of others. He couldn't listen to others and hear them for his own inner turmoil. Later, he wrote:

> The day was to come when I would break down the barriers and let the group see into myself . . . I had not trusted them initially to handle my feelings responsibly. I had given them additional reason to doubt and to disrespect my sentiments, and finally, I had become angry with them for not being respectful of my concerns. All of this I had wrought!

When George found the strength to share this with his fellows, they listened and heard him. In turn, George was able to *hear* the others in the group because their hearing and understanding relieved his inner struggles.

3. Another hearing barrier can result from being too emotionally involved with the person you are trying to hear. This is one reason family members who love each other very much have difficulty hearing at times. Family members have hopes for each other and expectations of one another. They fear for each other and

they hurt for one another. These very factors make it difficult for them to hear very clearly at times. In a family, we do listen in judgment and we do listen out of our *shared* inner struggles. It is natural, therefore, that this emotional involvement may become a barrier.

This emotional involvement can happen outside the family circle as well. It is possible to become too emotionally involved rather suddenly with one you are listening to and, forgetting for a moment, respond to your own emotions rather than hear what the other person is saying. This can happen between the best of friends. A young man came to me to discuss some personal problems. When I asked if he had gone to anyone for counseling and he said he had, I asked who he had gone to. He said, "Oh, when things get really bad, I talk them over with my girl friend. But lately, it hasn't helped." His emotional involvement with his girl friend became a barrier preventing her from hearing the depth of inner conflict and pain the young man was feeling.

It is paradoxical that to *hear* most clearly, we almost have to separate ourselves emotionally from the other person. It is to our advantage to be able to identify with the other—we identify strongly when we can "walk in our brother's moccasins." However, *over-identification* can be a barrier to hearing. Counseling with a rebellious teenage boy, I was aware of thinking of my own children and my relationship with them as he talked. This identification increased my desire to help; but momentarily I was listening and hearing myself rather than the young man speaking.

4. Barriers to hearing may be in the person speaking. They are not all limited to the listener. For various reasons, persons may speak as though they are *afraid* of being heard. Some speak so quietly they cannot easily be heard, others speak in a bored monotone and some use language that has the effect of blocking communication. In such instances the listener can only point out to the speaker the situation, such as, "I am trying very hard to hear you, but you are speaking so quietly I cannot."

We listen in order to hear; we want to hear in order to understand. Through understanding we can develop and nurture a caring relationship with other persons.

What It Means to Understand

There are different ways of understanding. Dr. Alfred Benjamin suggests three ways:[10] to understand *about* the other person; to understand the other person *through* my own feelings and experiences; to understand *with* the other person, or to understand what it is like to be that person. These represent different levels, from limited understanding to fuller understanding. The third kind, to understand *with* is obviously the most important and the most difficult in caring relationships.

To understand is to grasp the meaning of something or to comprehend the nature and significance of something. When this is applied to a person, we see that to understand means to grasp the nature and significance of a person's life situation at the moment we are listening to and hearing the person. The whole of the person's life situation is not involved—such understanding can only be partial and momentary. To understand is to momentarily enter the other person's world of experience and feeling through listening and hearing.

Such understanding is possible for caring persons—more possible than most of us dare to think. The *desire* to understand is the single most important factor in accomplishing it. This caring on the part of the listener is communicated to the person who speaks and enables the person to enter more fully into the relationship. Here again we see the active character of caring and listening applied to understanding. As I listen, wanting to hear and to understand, the effect upon my friend is to allow it to happen.

---

10. *The Helping Interview*. Houghton Mifflin, 1974, 2nd ed.

Wanting to understand, I make every effort to become aware of what it is like to be that other person. This requires two things of me, the listener. First, I must put aside my frames of reference. This third way of understanding is different from the second way, when I understand through my own feelings and experiences. This way of understanding depends upon freeing myself (as much as possible) from my own feelings and experiences in order to enter into the other person's world. Second, I strive for *empathy*. Empathy is not the same as sympathy. When I sympathize with you, I identify with you, and become as you are in feeling and perception. In empathy I retain my own distinctive self and you retain yours, but I understand your view of things and your response to life.

Charles had been caught in a robbery while purchasing milk in a convenience store. He had been forced to lie on the floor with bound hands and feet. The next day he told his friend Marty the frightening experience. "Marty, you just could never understand what it was like!" But the fact is that Marty was hearing his friend Charles and was emotionally going through the experience with him. As he listened, Marty was not relating what he heard to his own experience or his feelings about his own life (he had never been in such a situation), but he was responding as though he were there with Charles in those critical moments.

It is this quality of empathy that allows us to understand the difficult situations of others and to offer our support and strength. If we could understand only through identification, or sympathy, we would too often be so caught up in the crisis of the other person's life, we could not be effective as caring persons.

In addition to understanding "with" the other person, we understand through our own feelings and experiences. For example, surgical operations seem to be a common instance where this is done. "Let me tell you about *my* operation!" Having been through such an experience, you can sympathize with your friend who is preparing for it. This may be adequate and allow your caring to be expressed positively for your friend's sake.

Understanding *about* a person is often necessary. Before visiting a friend who is shut-in, it is important to know that she has no living close relative. You have begun to understand something essential in listening and hearing her.

In all three ways of understanding, the other person is the focus of our attention, the object of our thought. Alfred Benjamin proposes an interesting test for our listening for understanding.

> The test is this: If during the interview you can state in your own words what the interviewee has said and also convey to him in your own words the feelings he has expressed and he then accepts all this as emanating from him, there is an excellent chance that you have listened and understood him.[11]

This moving out of the self toward the other person to listen and to understand has particular meaning for the Christian caring person. It is not possible for the self-centered person; to focus outside self upon the other comes with too much difficulty. The Christian caring person cannot do it effortlessly or carelessly. But understanding *with* the other person is possible for us, and its positive outcomes in caring relationships are seldom fully realized.

What it Means to Accept

It is apparent that none of us can accept everyone, nor can we accept different persons equally. But acceptance is integral to the caring relationship. The love and grace of God brings to the human relationship a transcendent power. It is the power of the new creature or the new being.

11. *Ibid.*, p. 45.

This quality belongs to physical, emotional, and spiritual maturity. Physical and emotional maturity is necessary because of the way we learn, grow, and develop. The fact that human love is imperfect has been universally recognized. That imperfection is seen in one way parents communicate love to growing children. For the sake of control, discipline, and training, our children sometimes experience love as *conditional* upon their response. If they are "good" and do as they are told, they are rewarded by being accepted and loved. If they are "bad" and not obedient, they feel love and acceptance withheld from them. The growing person quickly learns that giving or withholding love is an important means of exercising power.

At least two bad learnings result from conditional love. First, that we are loved by what we *do* rather than who we *are*. (This seems to go against what Christians believe about God.) Second, love is learned as a means of control rather than a way of relating to another person. We have to relearn what the love of self really is and what the love of others means. We learn the new lesson in various ways. One of them is when we meet that person for the first time who says, "I love you because of what you are, not what you do!" A healthy marriage relationship does this for many persons.

Spiritual growth is involved as well. The Christian faith speaks directly and powerfully to our condition. We learn that the love of God is never conditional but always free and unconditional. We can learn this lesson gradually over time. It can also be realized suddenly with accompanying deep emotion and there results a new birth—the formation of a new person.

This quality of full acceptance is called *unconditional positive regard* by Dr. Carl Rogers:

> Actually it is only the experience of a relationship in which he is loved (something very close, I believe, to the theologians' *agape*) that the individual can begin to feel a dawning respect for, acceptance of, and finally, even a fondness for himself. It is as he can thus begin

> to sense himself as lovable and worthwhile, in spite of his mistakes, that he can begin to feel love and tenderness for others.[12]

For the Christian, the acceptance of self and others as lovable ultimately rests with our acceptance of God's love. Within that love, we see all human beings as having immeasurable worth. In coming to fully accept a friend, this kind of love becomes functional. This is what Christian caring is about.

Accepting a person is not the same as giving approval. We listen to hear and understand. We can do that and even *accept* the person without giving approval either to what is being said or to actions that are described. Most of us can confess thoughts or deeds which need forgiveness. Whoever hears the confession can understand, forgive, and accept us without condoning the actions or thoughts we confess. We seek to become that kind of friend, that kind of listener to those with whom we relate. It is a constant challenge to our habits of criticizing, judging, and disagreeing. Coming to full acceptance of a friend is accompanied by the acceptance of ourselves with imperfections, but also with hope. The hope is in becoming new. Caring relationships belong to that becoming, whether we are the listener or the speaker.

We listen to another person in order to hear;
We hear to understand;
We understand that we may fully accept other persons and ourselves.

---

12. *The Chicago Theological Seminary Review*. January 1956, p. 14.

But a Samaritan . . . came to where he was; and when he saw him, he had compassion, and went to him and bound up his wounds, pouring on oil and wine; then he set him on his own beast and brought him to an inn, and took care of him.

Luke 10:33,34

No one is so accursed by fate,
No one so utterly desolate,
But some heart, though unknown,
responds to his own.

Henry Wadsworth Longfellow

3

Caring Through Responding

How strange! I may listen to another person without speaking. I may hear and understand and not say anything. Yet, all the while, I am responding. To respond means to make a reply or to act in return. We are responding the moment we stop to listen to a friend in a caring way. We are responding non-verbally as we seek to understand, and by our manner communicate acceptance. These are all essential, basic ways of responding. Of course it becomes necessary to respond verbally as well. There are innumerable ways of responding in a caring relationship. Many different meanings can be conveyed. We choose our responses carefully and seek to make them meaningful and helpful for the persons to whom we listen as well as for ourselves.

The Focus of Response

As I listen carefully and empathetically to another person, my responses will take different orientation at different times. There are three orientations: my response will focus on the speaker, my response will focus on me, and my response will alternate between one and the other.

Responses Which Focus on the Speaker

As you listen to your friend, you do so understanding that he or she is responsible for self: thoughts, feelings, and actions. And you listen to your friend as an equal. Whatever your response, it is to reflect this way of listening, understanding, and relating to your friend. This way of responding sounds easy and natural. It is not as easy as it sounds. In the everyday round, we become more accustomed to focusing on ourselves than upon others. This carries over, without thinking, into a caring, listening relationship unless one is alert and determines not to do so. There are several ways in which a listener's response focuses upon the speaker.

1. One way is by *silence*. Your careful, empathetic silence is a response which can focus on your friend. Much of what you hear in careful listening can best be responded to in silence. Your silence can communicate sensitivity, understanding, and acceptance, and at times, it will communicate these more effectively than any words. One note of caution: the silence must represent your total self, present in thought and feeling. If you have lost your orientation upon your friend and your focus is on yourself or someone not present, your silence will communicate indifference.

2. Another response focusing upon your friend (speaker) is *any signal* that you hear and understand. Sometimes it is only a nod of the head. It might be "Um-hmm," or "I understand," or simply "Yes." These are all meant to convey permissiveness. They are a way of responding to encourage your friend to go on because you are going *with* him or her. The signal should not agree or disagree. It should not make a judgment or raise a question. It should convey the encouragement that comes with a continuing caring relationship. As you say "Um-hmm" or "I see," you should be aware of what your voice tone communicates as well. There are times when the person you are listening to may hear your response as questioning or criticizing. If it sounds something like,

"Um-HUMM!" you probably are criticizing! Every word we use and every sound we make carries meaning in a relationship, and we learn to become aware more fully of what the meaning is.

3. *Restatement* is an important way of responding which focuses upon the speaker. It is important because it conveys to your friend how clearly you are hearing. It is best not to try to say the exact words your friend uses. None of us likes to have another "parrot" what we say. At the same time, to change too many words can cause you to miss clearly where your friend is in thought and feeling. It may sound something like this:

> Your friend: When I got up to speak at our group meeting I just froze up—I got so scared!
>
> You: You are really afraid when you get up in front of people at our group meeting.
>
> Your friend: Yes, I guess I am afraid of something—I don't know what.

By restatement you enable your friend to hear what he or she has said; it is something like an echo. You have experienced the value of this when you are listened and responded to in this way. You hear yourself when you say it, but there is special help when you hear your listener say it too. You may even have thought, "Well, that is certainly what I said, but that is not exactly what I feel and think." When you realized that, you went on to change or add to it. The response in the foregoing illustration helped your friend to recognize the feeling of fear for what it was in that situation.

4. *Clarification* is another way of responding which still focuses upon the speaker. While restatement has a clarifying function in it, some responses are specifically made to assist the speaker to clarify feelings and thoughts. This is especially helpful when, under stress with conflicting feelings, your friend expresses varied feelings and thoughts all together. Here you must try to sort out predominant ideas and feelings you hear, and say them back concisely and clearly.

Your friend: I couldn't decide whether or not to go with him. He can be so nice and loving, then all at once he wants to run my life. I like him, but sometimes when we are on a date I can get so mad at him, then I feel sorry and let him run me around.

You: "You really like Bill, but he can be too bossy."

In a clarifying response, you probably will omit some things your friend has said. However, if you respond with what you hear to be the most important of the thoughts or feelings, your response helps your friend to clarify his or her situation.

Four ways of responding that clearly focus on the speaker which we have looked at are *silence, "Umhmm,"* *restatement* and *clarification*. As you begin to become a more careful listener, it is not expected that your every verbal response must be inwardly debated for a "right" selection. Rather, your sensitivity and experience gradually allow you to make the most appropriate responses.

Responses Which Focus on the Listener

When your response focuses on the speaker, the responsibility is fully with that person. In other responses, the listener begins to assume some responsibility *with* the speaker. Debate continues among counselors and therapists as to which is the most effective way of dealing with persons: in a "directive" way or a "non-directive" way. In human relationships both seem to be a normal part of the give and take. In a caring relationship, there is generally awareness and intention in which way we respond: how much responsibility the listener can and should take in the relationship.

In responses which focus on you, the listener, you are willing and able to respond by *explaining, encouraging, reassuring,* and *suggesting*. It is not that you take away your friend's responsibility, but you are clear about inserting your own judgments, ideas, decisions, and perceptions.

1. *Explanation* is a response which focuses on the listener. To explain is to make plain. For example, as you listen to your friend reveal personal events you may want to respond with an explanation of how you intend to listen and relate. You may say it something like this:

> I want you to know that anything you say will remain only between the two of us. I want to listen and to try to understand.

As you grow to understand a friend more, explanation can be a response that is helpful in various circumstances. This response is best used in dealing with things as they are—factual material and circumstances. For example, your friend may be sharing inner conflict over accepting an important responsibility in a favorite organization. You understand that in part the conflict is the result of your friend having incorrect information about the nature of the job which you know about. Your response is an explanation which allows your friend to resolve part of the inner conflict. This response is used selectively: when an explanation directly clarifies or enables the person to move forward toward a solution or decision.

2. *Encouragement* is another response that more fully centers on the listener than on the speaker. Caring persons want to be supportive. Our whole motivation to listen and to understand rests on this positive ground. We want to be helpful, and for most of us, giving encouragement is being helpful. It is natural for us to try to encourage a friend when we hear discouragement come through. Often, we try without knowing if our offering a few words of encouragement has really helped. It is important to know that giving encouragement to a friend may come more from your perspective, your frame of reference than from that of your friend. In a sense, to give encouragement is to influence your friend in a particular way. If it is

realistic and your friend can "buy into" the encouragement, it probably is a helpful response.

Your friend: Every day seems just like the one before. I seem to get discouraged so easily these days.

You: I understand. Yet, you have told me of friends whom you appreciate and that you are beginning to feel competent in your work. There must be things in your life you would not want to change very much.

Your friend: That's true.

Encouragement, as all other responses, must come out of the person's real life situation, and be based on something that the person experiences. As you listen to your friend, you may become aware that there is a basis for the friend to feel encouragement, but cannot see it at the moment. Your response is to uncover the basis for taking courage.

3. *Reassurance* also focuses on the listener and at first glance seems the same as encouragement. It is similar, but goes further in that the listener takes even more responsibility and speaks more out of his or her own perception. You may reassure your friend when you see, for example, more capacity for strength than he or she acknowledges.

Your friend: I think I will have to quit the job. It is much harder for me than I thought. I'll never get the hang of it.

You: I think you can do it. You said last week you felt much better about it when your supervisor said you were improving. They are not about to let you go, so why quit? You really have the ability if you want to stay with it.

Your friend: I would like to stay with the job. I suppose I want to master it too quickly.

Notice the influence inherent in your reassurance. Again, you do not want to take that much on yourself unless your knowledge allows you to do so with assurance that you speak realistically.

4. *Suggestion* is a response that more clearly focuses on the listener. As you make a suggestion to the friend, you are assuming more responsibility than in any of the previously discussed types of responses. It is often dangerous for us to give advice to our friends. The advice might be bad, and if the friend does not really believe the advice is possible, cannot implement it. Giving suggestions moves in the direction of giving advice, but need not be as strong. It leaves room for the other person to decide and not to follow the suggestion unless it is appropriate.

Your friend: I don't know what to do. Mary and Jim seem to be upset with us. We have been such good friends and we don't want to lose their friendship.

You: Let me make a suggestion. Could you telephone them, or write a note and tell them something like that? It might be worth a try.

Your friend: I would not want to call, but I can write a note. That's a good idea.

Responses Focusing Alternately Between the Speaker and Listener

Our responses in a caring relationship are many and varied. The larger number will center about the one to whom you are listening, with those responses centering upon you coming through in needed and appropriate times. In most instances, both you and your friend want him or her to retain responsibility for self, in thought and action. On the other hand, there are times when your insight, your understanding, your perception of your friend, offered in a genuine and non-authoritative manner, can be a helpful response.

Types of Responses

In considering the *focus* of response, the various *kinds* of responses appear. There are five different attitudes conveyed in a listener's responses. Howard Clinebell, Jr., identifies them as evaluative, interpretive, supportive, probing, and understanding. Clinebell writes,

> . . . an *evaluative* response is one which carries the counselor's value judgment; an *interpretive* response is one which intends to teach or explain the dynamics of a person's behavior (the "why"); a *supportive* response is one which seeks to reassure, inspire, or undergird a person; a *probing* response is one which questions; and an *understanding* response is one which reflects the counselee's feelings and attitudes.[13]

Because caring relationships beyond trained counselor and counselee relationship are being discussed here, the responses we are most interested in are encompassed by supportive, probing, and understanding responses. Untrained counselors will be slow to use evaluative or interpretive responses and will use them very selectively. However, many responses you make to a friend will be supportive and understanding, and sometimes probing.

Supportive Responses

Every person needs support and depends upon someone or something for it. The pastor has always been looked to in a congregation as a major source of support by many of the members. Beyond this, the network of caring relationships has also served as the basis of support for many persons. In their book, *Pastoral Care in Historical Perspective,* Clebsch and Jaekle point out that, "Tightly knit communities once furnished friends and neighbors who could stand by in moments of shock, whereas in a society on wheels the task of providing such sustenance to urban and

---

13. *Basic Types of Pastoral Counseling*. Abingdon, 1966, p. 72.

suburban people falls heavily on the clergy."[14] However, in most congregations, there can be a return to the more widespread practice of supportive, caring relationships among the members.

Many of our responses to others in caring relationships will be supportive ones. What is meant by "supportive"? Such responses include the following characteristics.[15]

1. Supportive responses are made to strengthen the other person.

2. Supportive responses are aimed at nurturing and sustaining a person.

3. Supportive responses seek to motivate the other person.

4. Supportive responses generally focus on the here and now.

5. Supportive responses are often action oriented, drawing the helper (listener) into a person's life situation more directly.

Much caring activity that goes on in a parish community can be described by these characteristics. Rallying around a family at a time of physical crisis or death is an example. The responses are action oriented, in the here and now, aimed at strengthening and sustaining the members of the family. The verbal responses in a conversation can also produce such outcomes. The person who cares, listening and responding, utilizes many of these characteristics.

The use of religious resources is a means of supportive response. Reading from the Bible, engaging in prayer, using devotional material—all are done to strengthen, sustain, and nurture. They are also utilized to motivate persons. Such responses are especially appropriate as we call upon the shut-in, hospitalized, convalescent, and those suffering grief and loss.

---

14. Aronson, 1975, p. 80.
15. Howard J. Clinebell, Jr., *Basic Types of Pastoral Counseling*, pp. 139-140.

Dangers in Supportive Responses

Even though various supportive responses are natural to the caring relationship and are of benefit in many situations, their use carries certain dangers. These should be noted and avoided.

1. Supportive responses can serve as "crutches" for some persons, slowing healing and retarding growth. Since supportive responses are focused more on the helper's perspective than on the speaker's or friend's, they may be used as ends in themselves rather than for change or growth. The person is content to have your support, rather than to use it in exercising his or her own strength for change and healing.
2. Supportive response can encourage dependency. Some persons needing help and support bring an unusual amount of dependency (upon others for their ongoing functioning) to the caring relationship. Too much support can encourage their dependency rather than help them to grow out of it.
3. Supportive responses can cause the helper to exercise too much control over the other person. Many of us like to be needed. When others come to depend upon us and love us for it, we may like the relationship to continue that way.

Emphasizing Strengths Through Supportive Responses

Modern life brings stress to all. There is stress from competition at work, stress in the family, stress from social relationships, stress from financial worry. Such pressure has the effect of showing up some weakness in most persons. There always seems to be someone around who will point out our weaknesses! If not, we are aware of them anyway.

Experiencing loss, failure, breakdown in relationships, persons are prone to give more attention to shortcomings than to their strengths. Perhaps the single most valuable outcome of a caring relationship is to reverse that tendency. It is to encourage a person to take account of his or her strengths in the face of challenge, to marshal them and to use them in dealing with the situation.

Probing Responses: The Use of Questions

As you listen to another person, it is not unusual for questions to come to mind. It is tempting to ask, "Why did you do that?" For most persons, "why?" means disapproval, and can interfere in the process. In talking with a counselor, the counselee said, "After I took my wife to the hospital for surgery, I took off and went fishing." The counselor said, "Why in the world did you do that?" The distraught husband replied, "I don't know *why*."

A "why" response is seldom as helpful as some other response. If a person knew *why* he or she did, felt, or thought something, there might be no need to talk it over with a friend.

How to Use Questions

If questions are to be used effectively as a response, they should be as open and broad as possible. That is, the questions should not be so closed as to elicit limited response. A closed question asks only for facts or incidents, such as, "How old are you?" A broad question, one that is open, invites the person to say more, to select what is most important to be expressed. "Do you like school?" is an open question, while "you like school, don't you?" is a closed one. If a question can be answered yes or no, it will provide little opportunity for conversational development.

It is important to ask single, not double questions. It is difficult to deal with more than one question at once, especially when under stress. Such a question poses more than one choice but asks the person to make only one choice. "Am I being helpful to you, are you learning more about yourself?" is a double question. The response to this would likely be, "I don't know!" One question at a time would allow the person better opportunity to answer. You might ask, "Are you learning more about yourself?" At least the person might feel like attempting an answer.

As a response, the question is better if it is indirect, rather than direct. An indirect question appears to be a statement because there is no question at the end. "It must be difficult to hold down two jobs," or "I wonder what it is like to be a twin." The indirect question has the open characteristic. It invites the speaker to talk more and to have open choices as to what is said.

When to Use Questions

There are times when a question is required. One is when you are unable to hear or to understand what your friend has said. "I didn't hear the last part. What did you say?" is an example. A question is also used to discover how you have been understood by your friend. "I have said several things; what have you understood me to say?" Another time to use a question is to help your friend clarify a thought or feeling. For example, "Are you saying you feel guilty when you have a good time?" Such a question can have the effect of helping your friend explore the thought or feeling further.

A question is used also when you need more information, such as, "When did you first begin to feel lonely?" or, "Have you been in the hospital for treatment before?" There are many occasions when such questions need to be asked when you are visiting in the hospital or in a retirement or convalescent home.

Finally, use a question in order to help your friend when he or she finds it difficult to continue, yet obviously has more to say. A direct, simple question like, "Would you like to say more?" can be the prompting that is needed. The indirect question might be effective here, such as, "I know it must be very hard for you to talk about this." The understanding and patience expressed this way can enable your friend to continue.

We may think of more questions to ask than are helpful. The listener must avoid asking one question after another, especially closed and direct questions. In answering such questions, your friend becomes more oriented to you and your need for information than to his or her concerns. Further, such a string of questions can condition short and comparatively meaningless answers which give your friend no relief but may contribute to tension and a feeling of helplessness.

Caring relationships call upon us to respond, and we learn to respond with care—care-fully! We choose the more helpful ones and respond with empathy, patience, and understanding. We choose our responses to enable our friends to maintain responsibility, to grow in self-understanding and effective Christian living. We respond in order to nurture the healing process. We respond out of our mutual need to love and to care.

Counseling "By the Way"

"Do you have a minute? I would like to talk with you." This is often how it begins. You might be preparing to go hunting with a friend, or "run into" a friend while shopping, or just answering the telephone. The chance encounter as well as the planned meeting provides caring persons with opportunity to stop, listen, and to respond. It seems that some of the most important listening and responding takes place "by the way."

There are many persons in congregations with whom friends feel free to talk and share anxieties. Some of them have said to me, "People seem to trust me and I want to be of help, but I am not trained. I don't know if I am doing them a favor or not." The more training we have to do counseling, the better. As lay counselors, we are not trained and competent to do what professional counselors can do. However, the exercise of a caring relationship in listening empathetically and responding with love and concern is a form of counseling. In many instances, perceptive and empathetic persons are being helpful and render a significant service to their friends.

So this counseling "by the way" is not understood as professional counseling nor should it take its place. This counseling is understood as exercising the caring relationship in many ways, including significant and therapeutic conversation. No counseling is simply giving advice or telling another person what to do in a puzzling situation. This counseling is the exercise of a mutually caring relationship, usually between equals, in which one is able to listen, understand, accept, and respond to the other for his or her nurture and healing.

Tom and Will met at the car wash and, while waiting, began to visit. Tom, noticing Will was preoccupied, asked if everything was all right.

"Frankly, no," Will said. "My son has upset me and we had a run-in about ten minutes ago. I guess I haven't gotten over it yet."

Tom listened and Will was able to work through some feelings and come to a decision as to how to re-establish communication with his son.

Most of us have the opportunity to counsel "by the way." Some avoid it, some embrace it. As in other human relationships, our desire is to be sincere, genuine, and loving. This carries significant responsibility. In this spirit, we are able to respond when a friend says, "Oh, by the way, do you have a minute? I would like to talk with you."

Guidelines for Counseling "By the Way"

1. Remember that a person shares life's struggles with another because of his or her need for understanding, acceptance, and support. If you can listen carefully and empathetically, you can become an instrument for the person's needs to be met.

2. Be a careful listener. Stay with your friend in feeling and idea. Hear what is being said, giving signals that you are hearing. Do not ask questions that divert the person until it is clear what he or she is hurting about. Do not be afraid of silence as long as you are attentive. Choose your responses carefully, making certain they will further the conversation with clarity and meaning.

3. Do not offer advice, such as, "If I were you, I would. . . ." If your friend asks you what to do, don't hesitate to say, "I really cannot say, but by talking this over with me, perhaps you can decide for yourself." Even though it appears clear to you that your friend should take a particular action or make a certain decision, remember that your making the decision does not mean that your friend can live with it.

4. Don't hesitate to answer direct questions concerning your friend's concerns with "I don't know." This may give you an opening to suggest that your friend seek professional help. This may be the finest service you can give. Your assurance that persons especially trained to help your friend are available may be what is needed.

5. Reassure your friend that you want to continue to listen, even though you will not attempt to decide for him or her. Let your friend know that what he or she chooses to tell you remains only with the two of you.

6. After your friend has communicated the nature of the hurt, you may be able to assist him or her to think through and evaluate the situation. Your responses may well encourage the person to make another step toward seeking professional help if that is needed. If not, your responses may supply your friend with the understanding and support that is sufficient.

7. Discourage talking with your friend for too long a period at one time. Both of you can get emotionally and physically tired. Usually, one hour is enough. When you are aware of the time, simply say, "We really should not talk longer than a few minutes more now; we can talk another time." There are exceptions, of course, when it is better to complete a conversation

rather than to interrupt it. However, it is often preferable to have several shorter periods than one or two long, exhausting sessions. The more fatigued you and your friend become, the less possibility there is for learning and change to take place.

8. When the time is up, you may need to bring the conversation to a close. Try to pick up on a positive note struck during the talk in order that your friend can go away with basis for encouragement. Review it, offering your reassurance. If your friend does not ask first, you may ask when he or she would like to talk again. Sometimes the person will say, "No, this has helped a lot; I don't need to talk again."

9. In the event your friend shows confusion or deep discouragement (depression), offer to help get an appointment with a counselor or physician. Or you may offer to call the pastor. Sometimes you can offer to accompany your friend for an appointment.

10. If your friend is depressed and alone, and you cannot stay with him or her, assist in finding someone your friend can stay with until an appointment with a professional counselor can be kept.

11. As you leave, express your gratitude for sharing with your friend and briefly reiterate your loving concern.

12. Take your cue from your friend for praying or reading scripture or devotional resources. Let your friend speak the prayer or share the leadership. Follow the need and wish of your friend.

As with all guidelines, these are too brief and can never be adequate in all situations. They are a beginning. They are not to be followed as steps to be achieved, but as clues and directions to help chart the way. Your loving spirit, along with openness to develop your skill, is the means for extending caring relationships.

Referral: A Caring Response

A cardinal rule for helping persons should be, "I will not attempt to counsel someone if I know someone else is available who can do it better." Unfortunately, the rule is not always followed. The key for caring persons is in the phrase, "If I know someone else is available." Many persons are in need of a caring listener. Some will seek professional help; some will not.

Referral is a caring response. First, it is so because of your concern. You want your friend to have help appropriate to the need. Second, because of the trust your friend has placed in you, you can use your ability and influence to help make referral possible.

The caring relationship is not terminated with referral. Your interest and concern continues while your friend finds appropriate help from a professionally trained person. Your support and encouragement often can be crucial in your friend's continuing growth and healing.

There are many examples of referral through a caring relationship.

—The parents of a boy were referred to a university hearing clinic when they discovered his trouble in school stemmed from impaired hearing.

—An elderly couple were referred to a church-sponsored housing project when they could no longer keep their home.

—A laboring man was referred to a physician when he became too depressed to hold his job.

—A middle-aged couple were referred to a marriage counselor when they became helpless to halt a deteriorating relationship.

—A college student was referred to a drug treatment center when he failed in his studies.

All of these persons are representative of persons you know and worship with in church. They are your neighbors and your fellow workers. Like you, they have specific needs which demand specific care and treatment. The pastor often is aware of such needs but cannot know of them all. Many caring Christians come to know of such needs and can respond appropriately.

Guidelines for Referral

1. Be sensitive to your friend's needs and decide if you can meet them. If you are uncertain, wait until the situation clarifies.

2. When you are certain that you should refer your friend to someone else, inform yourself as to who is available. The pastor is your first resource, either as the one to see your friend or to suggest other resources. Many persons needing help will simply be referred to the pastor.

3. If possible, be prepared to offer your friend more than one option for referral. For example, if your friend has no family physician, suggest the names of two or three, from which the choice can be made.

4. Offer to help contact the referral source, if necessary.

5. Check to see when an appointment is made that your friend can keep it. You can assist with transportation, baby-sitting, or other matters that can complicate keeping appointments.

6. Call to inquire how the appointment went and to offer your encouragement. (Remember that in counseling and other therapeutic treatment, as well as in physical treatment, time is required for results to appear.)

It is true that in many communities there are limited resources for helping persons. The lack of money for such service is often an issue. However, there are many agencies, county, state and federal, as well as private agencies, that provide services for minimal fees.[16] County and community welfare offices are often a source of information, as well as such professional persons in the community as ministers, physicians, attorneys, and social workers.

You can be assured that as a vital link between a person in need and a person who can render competent treatment, you are fulfilling a caring relationship.

---

16. Marcus D. Bryant and Charles F. Kemp, *The Church and Community Resources*. Bethany Press, 1977.

. . . I was sick and you visited me, I was in prison and you came to me.

Matthew 25:36b

Faith has to do with the basis, the ground on which we stand.

Hope is reaching out for something to come.

Love is just being there and acting.

Emil Brunner

4

Caring Through Visitation—I

Visitation is an act of Christian love; it is "being there and acting." As Christian persons, we reach out to others because of our identity. Our relationship to God, in which we are known and loved by our Creator, frames our relationship with other persons. We also reach out to others because we are part of the community of faith, hope, and love—the church. As an act of Christian love, visitation is a means whereby the Christian can be fully present with others in most meaningful ways. Emil Brunner says, "Therefore we can be truly human only in communion with our fellow men. And that is exactly what is lacking in us; we are never really present with our fellow men."[17]

The Christian visitor becomes the embodiment of a caring community of faith. Nowhere can one person be more present with another than when the other is suffering illness, or when alone and helpless, or when locked behind steel doors.

Visitation is also an art. Art is defined as "the activity of creating beautiful things."[18] Visiting a person in

---

17. *Faith, Hope and Love*. Westminster, 1951, p. 72.
18. *American Heritage Dictionary of the English Language*. Dell, 1970.

need gives the visitor an opportunity for a creative expression which is indeed personal and unique. To go to a person in need is in itself a potentially creative act. The reaching out of one human being to another always has within it the potential for "beautiful things." Beyond this, the visitor has the opportunity to further Christian relationship in a unique way.

A member of a church Koinonia (sharing) group went to the hospital for surgery. The other members could not visit, so they cut the shapes of their hands from colorful felt cloth, placed them on a banner-shaped cloth, and had one of their fellows take it to the hospital. The patient felt the unique "reaching out" of each of those hands.

Art can also be defined as any practical skill. Visitation does involve the exercise of some skills in order that the person being visited may be helped and not harmed. These skills are not difficult for caring persons. They come easily and naturally for most persons. However, there is a need to have some specific information, a need to do some planning, and a need to follow some basic guidelines.

Visiting the Homebound

The homebound person, or "shut-in," is one whose life is limited to house, wheelchair, or bed. This can be a temporary limitation, or one which is permanent for the life of a person.

Mr. Whitman was a seventy-three-year-old retired businessman who lived with his daughter and son-in-law. He was an enthusiastic church member and officer until crippling arthritis made him homebound. He was almost entirely confined to a wheelchair and his bed. His family gave him loving care, but he greatly missed his active life, including his church work.

Jim was fifteen his last birthday, the youngest of three children. An older brother and sister had married and moved away, and now Jim was left with his parents. Jim was able to leave the house only for automobile rides, because he was severely retarded, crippled, and could not speak. He seemed to enjoy seeing visitors, but it was difficult to know how much he understood.

Mrs. Betty Lisle was thirty-four and the mother of two children, Janie, seven, and Billy, four. Betty suffered from a serious heart condition and her activity had to be limited, so she could not attend church school and worship with her family. She planned to get back some day, and also to be able to do her own housework.

What Mr. Whitman, Jim, and Betty Lisle had in common was too much time and too little activity, the need for companionship, understanding, and encouragement. Loneliness especially is the experience of the homebound. In his book, *Loneliness,* Clark Moustakas writes, "Being lonely is such a total, direct, vivid experience, so deeply felt, so startlingly different, that there is no room for any other perception, feeling, or awareness."[19]

The caring visitor comes to Mr. Whitman, Jim, and Betty Lisle to share the depth of that loneliness, to bring each of them into the presence of an extended world, to share faith, hope, and love. Many of us become so apprehensive about our inadequacies, we lose sight of our opportunity for such service. Our feelings of inadequacy, our fear of the unknown, our fear of failing or of being a burden on others, all can be natural feelings. However, they need not stand in the way of participating in visitation. Rather, they can lessen our fears and enable us to grow as persons.

Guidelines for Homebound Visitation

1. Prepare for your visit. If possible, seek some basic information about the homebound person, such as, general health, reasons for being homebound, who

---

19. *Loneliness*. p. 8.

the person lives with, who has called from the church. It is important to telephone ahead and ask for a good time to call. Sometimes, it is necessary to ask how to enter the house or apartment because the homebound person may be alone for brief periods.

Decide what inspirational or devotional material to take, either to use or to leave with the person. Many churches have literature for this special purpose. Allow yourself adequate time for an unhurried visit (not necessarily long). Careful preparations enable you to give primary attention to the other person rather than to yourself.

2. Introduce yourself. In most instances, the shut-in person cannot answer the door, so it is important for you to be known to others in the home. You may also need to introduce yourself to the homebound person. As you do so, be sensitive to the person's physical condition. Shake hands if the person offers, but remember that a weak person does not enjoy a hearty handshake. On the other hand, the gentle touch of a caring person can be healing.

3. Invite the person to tell you about him or her self. An example for an older person might be, "I understand you are a charter member of our church." Many times you will not need to take the initiative, for the other person will want to talk. In the event the person cannot speak or does so with difficulty, you may need to speak for both of you. However, this does not mean you talk all the time. Moments of silence are not only necessary but desirable. Sharing information from church life or of mutual friends can be helpful. Reading aloud from the Bible or other literature is often appreciated.

Mrs. Estelle Blackman, who was in her late fifties, was confined to her bed and wheelchair with multiple sclerosis. She could speak only with great difficulty and very slowly. It embarrassed her to take the visitor's time listening to her laborious speech. The visitor listened and responded, periodically suggesting they take time to rest. Then the visitor read favorite passages from the Bible, closing with a classic prayer of comfort and strength.

4. Listen appreciatively. Most of the time, you need to speak only briefly. Then it is best to respond directly to the leads the other person gives you. For example, the person might say, "I am lonely these days." Your response might be, "You miss being with new people every day." The shut-in can reflect on that and may say, "Yes, that's it! I enjoyed meeting new people every day for so long in my work, and I miss that very much."

To listen appreciatively is to give attention to what is being said and the feelings with it, then to respond directly to that rather than to something else you might be reminded of. This is difficult when the person complains. To respond too directly to it might encourage the complaining. It is better to communicate your concern and let the person know you hear what is being said. Something like, "I think I can understand," is sufficient. As you listen, you bring your whole self into presence with the other person, thinking and feeling with him or her. Then your response is not to teach or to correct, but to show love and understanding.

5. Respond directly to the positive feelings. This helps the person realize how important the positive feelings are. For example, the shut-in person might say, "I am so grateful for my niece." Your response might be, "It is a fine home she shares with you, isn't it?" The positive, strong feelings and attitudes need to be encouraged and given support. This is necessary because with illness and handicaps it is natural for negative feelings to be expressed. They need to find expression for the person to regain health and wholeness. However, when the positive is real and finds expression, it needs recognition.

6. Be aware of the passage of time. The length of the visit varies as to the personal situation of the shut-in. If there is illness and/or pain, the visit might be as short as five or ten minutes. If the person is not uncomfortable, the visit might be from thirty minutes to an hour in length. When you feel it is right to end the

visit, mention this to the person, then get up and leave promptly. Be careful not to promise to return unless it is possible for you to do so.

7. If the person has asked for prayer or the reading of scripture, or you feel it would be welcome, offer it. You may also leave some devotional resources with the person. It is best if you use a prayer you have prepared in advance, but one in which can be incorporated thoughts arising from the visit. There are always times when you want to offer an extemporaneous prayer when it may be best to do so. Usually the choice of scripture is also done in advance unless the person requests special passages to be read. Sections from the Psalms which lift up God's love and faithfulness and from the Gospels are especially appropriate biblical sources.

8. Before leaving, share something simply and briefly as to what the visit has meant to you. Few persons make visits to persons in need without finding comfort and strength for themselves they were not expecting. Sometimes the visitor speaks only to others after leaving the shut-in person. It is best shared with the person you have come to visit. After one person spent thirty minutes with an elderly woman who loved the church, the visitor said to her, "You have helped me to feel differently about the church; your love for it is so real." Often, the person being helped can help the helper! This needs to be shared in the Christian relationship.

Visiting the Hospitalized Person

Physical illness dramatically changes one's life. Whether the illness is *acute*, lasting not more than six to eight weeks, or *chronic*, generally lasting longer, one's freedom of movement and physical strength is reduced. This is difficult for most of us to accept and adjust to. Persons who have been able to care for themselves become dependent upon others, at times for even intimate bodily functions. The forced inactivity has caused time to weigh heavily, in contrast to other days when the person never had time for all the activity.

In addition, physical pain and the discomfort of medical treatment sometimes leave the person helpless and bewildered. For some, the sharpness of pain may be a new experience. For others, pain may be an old acquaintance, one they may or may not have been able to accept. In his book, *People in Pain,*[20] Mark Zborowski points out that certain life-styles have an influence on how persons cope with physical pain. For example, a man who has known hard physical labor all his life might approach his pain as "tough luck" to be endured uncomplainingly, whereas a person who has been encouraged to express many feelings while growing up will probably need to express them when experiencing pain. Both are struggling—one needs to express the struggle more than the other.

Like much else in life, how we experience physical illness is unique to each person. A sensation painful to one may not be to another. Yet, persons suffering physical illness do respond to their changed condition emotionally as well. Many times, the emotional response can be as important to the person's recovery and well-being as is the physical disorder. The hospital visitor cannot be expected to be aware of them all. However, being aware of some emotional responses that are commonly encountered can be helpful.

Hospital patients can experience fear, loneliness, anger, and guilt. Any of these can be normal responses to physical illness unless they become exaggerated. Fear is often the result of facing unusual new experiences. This is especially true when one's safety and welfare are threatened. Most persons fear pain and death. In most instances, to be hospitalized does not mean death or necessarily great pain. Yet, hospitalization brings anxiety to many persons and for some, fear is strong until health gradually returns.

---

20. *People in Pain*. Jossey-Bass, Inc., 1969, pp. 1-15.

A forty-five-year-old minister prepared to check into the hospital for what is considered "routine" surgery. Gene realized no surgery could be "minor" for him, but his operation had been described by his physician as rather "routine." He had never been a patient in the hospital. Yet he had been making pastoral visits to parishioners in hospitals for nearly twenty years. He felt well physically and emotionally and made his preparations with confidence, anticipating that now he would experience what his friends had. It was not until the nurses and attendants began preparing him for surgery the night before that he felt that first pang of fear. Several questions came to him: How will I tolerate the anesthesia, the operation? Will this really be routine? Am I prepared for any change in my present or future? As he answered them for himself, he thought of those he had visited so many times.

Loneliness is common among hospital patients at one moment or another. It can come to one in the middle of the night, just before surgery, or in long periods of convalescence. It comes as one realizes most clearly how life and death are so personal and individual after all. Russell Dicks points out in his book, *When You Call on the Sick,* "The need for companionship, for stimulus, for entertainment, for occupation is probably the greatest *spiritual* need of the convalescent; this is beyond his need of good medical nursing and dietary care."[21] Dicks is referring here both to loneliness and boredom. They often go hand in hand, especially for those with long hospitalizations.

Rachel White, a talented and effervescent redhead was the regional director for a national youth organization. She traveled a great deal and was an effective professional person in much demand. Late at night, during a long drive from one appointment to another, she was nearly killed in an automobile accident. There followed a long hospitalization with a series of operations, almost constant pain, and little promise for full recovery. Her pastor was faithful during the days and

21. *When You Call on the Sick*. Harper & Row, 1938, p. 6.

nights of crisis and then later helped to meet her need for recovery of her accustomed mental stimulation. Many persons in the hospital feel the same loneliness and boredom when faced with the sudden lack of mental activity and meaningful occupation.

Hospitalized patients can experience anger. Often the anger is unexpressed directly but is present nevertheless. Dr. Elizabeth Kubler-Ross' studies of death and dying have identified five stages in the process of dying. She relates the "bargaining" stage to persons experiencing pain. We each bargain in different ways, but a person in pain might pray silently, "God, let this pain pass and I will never again forget you." The very bargaining can be a form of the expression of anger—anger at God, life, self, and/or others.

Chaplain Ronald L. Clark found this to be true among hospital patients he serves.[22] Most persons in pain ask, "Why me?" and often come to view their illness as some form of God's punishment or conclude that God "really doesn't care about me." Many of us have had such thoughts but do not want to utter them. The feeling may be there, however, and we struggle to find other explanations to put our anger aside. It is not wrong or sinful to feel such anger when one is struggling against illness and pain. Many attempt to overcome it silently and alone, while others grasp for the comfort of a loving and understanding listener.

Will Johnson was dying of cancer. Although in his forties, he was just underway in his profession as a college teacher. With a family, the long preparation had been difficult but his goals were now beginning to be realized. He was a Christian man and a loving person, though it was difficult for him to express his love openly. "How could something like this happen?" he asked. The anger at the injustice was there—how could he express it acceptably to himself and others? There was no acceptable way to him, it seemed, so

22. *Ministering to Persons in Pain*. Unpublished Th.M. thesis, Brite Divinity School, Texas Christian University, Fort Worth, Texas, 1976, p. 33.

it stayed there, underneath the pain and discomfort of treatment. Those who loved him suffered with him as he struggled with the meaning of his pain, illness, and eventual death. His visiting friends were faithful and by their presence demonstrated the meaning of love in the presence of approaching death.

Jan was a bright teenager who discovered her eyesight was failing and the tests confirmed approaching blindness. Why shouldn't she be angry? Why should this happen to her, especially now? Crying, she was able to vent the anger at her momentary helplessness. The resiliency of youthful strength and her determination to use mind and ability saw her through the crisis. The anger drained; she could marshal her strength to deal with the day and the future. The presence of loving and understanding friends, there to receive the anger, accept it, and stand with the suffering young woman made a significant and lasting difference.

Guilt is not unfamiliar to many of us when we become ill. Sometimes we just can't put our finger on why we feel guilty for being sick. In the study of persons in pain referred to earlier, Chaplain Clark found that "many patients reflected an attitude of a God who was punishing them through pain for their 'sins' or for some reason of which they were unaware."[23] Some of us feel guilt and really don't relate it consciously to God at all. One woman who discovered she felt guilty every time she became ill, even with minor ailments, described how as a child whenever she caught cold or had to stay home from school for illness, her mother would lecture her on what she had done wrong to become ill. She had grown up believing that a person becomes ill only by being careless and ineffectual.

Similar feelings are expressed by others from their hospital beds. "If I had just done this or that differently, perhaps I wouldn't have gotten sick." Of course, the guilt is stronger following accidents. "I should not have gone out in the car today, and this would not have happened. I was wrong to do that."

---

23. *Ministering to Persons in Pain*. p. 34.

Kent Williamson was twenty-seven and excited. He had designed and was building a modest skateboard park. In the late fifties he had been one of the early skateboard enthusiasts but had only the streets to skate in. Now he also could ride in a park made for skateboarding. The park was opened and all went well for a few days. He was getting the feel for it again. Then, turning at the top of the concrete bowl, he felt his leg give way under him. In the hospital, he felt all the emotions: fear, anger, guilt, and loneliness. "Why did this have to happen now, when I am broke?" "If I had not made that run, or turned the way I did!" "I think I will have to sell the park; I never should have gotten into this in the first place!" "I'm glad you came—this place is getting to me." The visitor was empathetic—she understood. The visitor could not help change the circumstances resulting in feelings of fear, failure, anger, and guilt. The visitor could be present and listen and care.

Guidelines for Hospital Visitation

1. Before you go to the hospital, make some preparations. It is helpful to know why the person is in the hospital. The pastor is often the source of needed information. There are several reasons for contacting the pastor before making a visit. The pastor may want to know who is visiting from the church and can suggest appropriate times to visit. Also, the pastor often has other helpful information, such as the family who may be visiting.

You will also want to choose what to take in the way of devotional material and perhaps a simple gift. Some visitors like to prepare a prayer in advance to ensure the most helpful expression. It is also wise to take a blank card on which to leave a message with the patient, if necessary.

2. You should visit during regular hospital visiting hours. Some hospitals have more liberal visiting

policies than others; however, both for the patient and the hospital staff, a visit should be made at expected times.

3. Get the room number by telephoning ahead or by asking at the reception desk.

4. Knock before entering. The door may be closed or nearly closed. If there is no answer or a notice that the patient is not to be disturbed, inquire at the nursing station if the patient can receive visitors.

5. If you cannot visit the patient, write a brief message on the card to leave with the nurse for delivery to the patient.

6. Unless you are known by the patient, introduce yourself. Even if you and the patient are from the same church, you may want to indicate you are there both as a friend and as a representative of your church fellowship.

7. Expect to limit your call to ten minutes or less. This is a general rule and can apply almost universally. There are some exceptions, of course, but visits should seldom last more than twenty minutes. Take off your hat and coat so that your visit does not seem rushed.

8. If invited to sit down and a chair is available, do so, but do not sit on the bed. If you need to stand, try not to show discomfort or that you are in a hurry. Try to position yourself so the patient can see you easily without facing bright light. If someone else is in the room when you arrive and you are offered a chair, it is better to accept it than to discuss who will stand and sit. Or, "I can stand comfortably, thank you," may be sufficient.

9. Remember that you do not need to do all the talking. After saying something like, "I am very glad to see you," wait for the other person to speak. Listen not only to the words but the feelings in them. It is best to avoid arguing or giving advice. Sometimes a visitor can get drawn into telling his or her own personal story of an illness. This should not be done. Comments like "I understand" or "I have felt the same way" or nodding your head yes is sufficient.

10. Avoid being drawn into speculation about your friend's physical condition, medical or hospital procedure. Your call can be supportive of the healing process if you do not contribute to your friend's fear or lack of confidence in it. It is best not to encourage the patient to list symptoms or complaints. On the other hand, if the patient says something like, "I have no one to talk with and I must tell you this," listen carefully and empathetically.

11. If you ask how you can help, be prepared to run an errand or make a telephone call or tell a nurse of some kind of need. It is best not to become a "go-between" with the attending physician. However, you can say, "I will tell the nurse that you want to talk with your physician." Because hospital care is so thorough, most persons will respond to your offer of help by saying, "No, thank you, I have everything I need." However, asking your friend and hearing the response sometimes encourages the person to verbalize some personal spiritual needs.

12. Express your friendship and your concern as personally as possible. If the patient can speak comfortably, ask about his or her family, friends, hobbies, or what is being read. The patient needs to exercise the mind and to range beyond the present condition in thought and conversation. Of course, pain and medication will prevent much of this and you will understand any limitations the patient has.

13. After about eight or nine minutes, mention that you must be going. Express your hope and confidence in the welfare and comfort of the patient. If the person asks for scripture reading and/or prayer, or if you know it would be welcome, read the short passages you have prepared. Have a brief prayer which can well include thanksgiving, praise, and petition for strength of the patient, the healing grace of God, the healing skills of the physicians and nurses, and the caring of friends and relatives.

14. Say goodbye and leave promptly; do not linger at the door. Only shake hands if the patient shows a desire. Rather, place your hand on the shoulder or

arm (only if the person is not in pain) lightly and briefly. The healing touch of a loving person is most comforting to the ill person.

Although these guidelines are not comprehensive and always appropriate, in many instances, they can be helpful and can suggest variations a visitor might make. What is important is that the visit is planned and carried out with the welfare of the patient in mind. Other goals or tasks can be accomplished at other times.

Visiting the Nursing Home Resident

While approximately 80 percent of the elderly live in their own homes or those of relatives until death comes, research shows that 20 percent of all people in our country over sixty-five years of age spend some time or end their years in nursing homes.[24] In 1970, there were over twenty-three thousand nursing homes of all types in the United States.[25] Most congregations have members who reside in nursing homes. For some elderly persons, a time comes when they can no longer care for themselves or their families cannot care for them, and they must move into a home.

Lee and Ralph were just a few years from retirement, and both of them worked. Ralph's eighty-nine-year-old father had been living with them in their small home. For a time, he could stay alone safely during the day when both Lee and Ralph were at work. But now, suffering from loss of memory and physical incapacities, he could no longer be left alone. Ralph reluctantly found the best nursing home they could afford and moved his father into it. They visit him two or three times a week.

---

24. *That Thy Days May Be Long in the Good Land: A Guide to Aging*, Programs for Synagogues, Synagogue Council of America, 1975, pp. 79-81.
25. Gordon Moss and Walter Moss, editors, *Growing Old*. Pocket Books, 1975, p. 63.

There are generally three kinds of nursing homes, depending upon the kind of service they offer.[26] (1) Those which provide skilled nursing and medical attention constantly. Medicare may pay for the costs in these homes. (2) Those which can provide long-term nursing care for chronically ill or disabled persons who do not require constant medical supervision. Costs in these homes are covered by Medicaid, but not Medicare. (3) Those which provide room and board and services such as aid in dressing and personal hygiene.

The visitor in a nursing home will find the same wide variety of conditions and needs among the residents as when visiting the homebound or a person in the hospital. Age and physical condition as well as emotional stability and outlook vary widely. Some who enter nursing homes feel rejected by family and society. The greatest difficulty faced by most residents is in giving up their own homes and the relative freedom of living alone. The move into the nursing home results both in the loss of personal possessions gathered during a lifetime and the loss of the sense of worth or belonging. Some who lived in their own homes were alone before, but others who have been accustomed to the company of family or close friends feel sharply the relative loneliness of the nursing home.

A common problem for the aged is the increase of chronic physical ailments. Among nursing home residents, chronic conditions average four or five per person. These can include heart disease, arthritis, diabetes, and digestive disorders. Aging usually results in a decline in several of the five senses, especially vision and hearing. This can be true for taste and smell as well. Also, the sensitivity to pain may decrease with age. Other common characteristics include the slowing of reaction time. More time is needed to think, speak, and respond. Loss of memory is not unusual among the elderly. There is a tendency to be

26. *Ibid*. p. 62.

able to retain memories from the distant past while forgetting more recent events and experiences. This is why a visitor felt sadness and anger when the elderly resident said, "I am so glad you came, no one ever comes to see me. My daughter hasn't been to see me in over a year." Fortunately, the next day the visitor learned from a mutual friend that the daughter visits her mother in the nursing home every weekend. At the same time, the resident could recall with clarity experiences from her life twenty or thirty years earlier.

As in their earlier years, the elderly person can suffer from a number of emotional disorders. Among the most common are hypochondria (imagined physical symptoms) and depression. As with persons in other age groups, hypochondria serves the purpose of shifting anxiety from one life concern to a less threatening physical one. For example, the elderly person who feels neglected, isolated, or suffers criticism, develops physical complaints as a means of dealing with the situation.

Depression among the aged is also a common condition. This is usually a response to the significant loss the person has experienced: loss of health, career, spouse, and other family relationships; loss of home, social, and economic status; and the loss of self-esteem. Any one of these losses can result in a depressive reaction in persons, and in the elderly person they often come closely together and are cumulative.

While life in a nursing home can be discouraging and present problems for the resident, there are positive factors as well. In her book, *The Nursing Home Visitor,*[27] Frances Faunce expresses the belief that life in a nursing home can be interesting and maturing for a person. Positive attitudes on the part of the resident, the family, and friends can be crucial in supporting the resident's morale and outlook.

The caring Christian goes to the nursing home with realistic expectations, both as to the environment and the persons who live there. The visitor also goes

27. Abingdon Press, 1969.

expecting to make and maintain personal friendships growing out of a special understanding of the new friend's needs. At the heart of those needs is often the need for a rich and continuing religious experience.

Research has shown that there is a higher incidence in the belief in God among the aged and that they place more importance on the devotional life.[28] Robert Havighurst notes that "In the spiritual sphere there is perhaps no necessary shrinking of the boundaries, and perhaps there is even a widening of them."[29]

As Erik Erikson has shown in delineating the eight stages of life, the last stage is one in which the person's task is to come to grips realistically with one's whole life and to find completion and meaning in it.[30] This always involves some struggle and for some it is a very difficult one. Those who are able to bring a meaningful Christian faith to their advancing age are those most likely to be able to find this "wholeness."

Guidelines for Visiting the Nursing Home Resident

1. Learn as much general information about the resident as possible. Available information will vary from name and address to rather extensive information including age, prior occupation, family members, and how long the resident has been in the home. Choose a time to visit during regular visiting hours and, if possible, introduce yourself to a staff member. If your visiting becomes regular, it is helpful to be recognized by the staff.

2. Make clear to the resident who you are and the church you attend. When the person you visit belongs

28. Matilda W. Riley and Anne Foner, et. al., *Aging and Society, Vol. 1: An Inventory of Research Findings*, Russell Sage Foundation, 1968.
29. *Developmental Tasks and Education*. 2nd ed., McKay, 1952, pp. 72-3.
30. *Childhood and Society*. W. W. Norton, 1950, p. 275.

to another church, tell the person how you came to make this visit.

3. Touching is especially helpful to the nursing home resident. Greet him or her with a warm smile and handshake or a gentle touch on the arm or shoulder.

4. Take notice of where you find the resident; one may be in a wheelchair in the lounge area, another may be in bed, another may be walking down the hall. Ask the person where he or she can be comfortable while you visit.

5. Encourage the resident to talk about himself or herself—friends in the home, family, church relationships, and other topics comfortable for the resident to speak of. Share your ideas and experiences where appropriate so that your expectation to benefit from that person's life and experience will emerge.

6. Make your visit open-ended and be ready to close the visit at the convenience of the resident. It is usually appropriate to ask if a person is growing weary or needs to rest.

7. Share with the person briefly how your faith and/or church experience is important to you, then ask the person to share with you in similar ways. You and your friend can agree upon a devotional time together. (This may mean a change in location for the visit.) You will have brought devotional material which not only can be used in the visit but also left with the friend.

8. You can offer to perform various helpful tasks. This may not be done on the first visit, but later ones. You might write a letter, sew on a button, or run an errand to the drugstore. However, you need to avoid overdoing the "taking care of" posture with the friend. The relationship to be developed is the one most helpful to the other person and to you if there is mutual benefit.

9. You can make the best judgment as to how long the visit must be. Your first visit may be shorter because of your own anxiety. As you become more

comfortable and the relationship develops, the visit probably will be longer.

10. In most instances, the person will invite you to return. Do not be hurt or alarmed if this does not happen. It is preferable, of course, if there is mutual agreement as to when the next visit can take place. You can respond to the request that you write or telephone, or you can make the offer to do so. (Sometimes, a resident does not have access to a telephone.)

11. As in a visit to the shut-in, share with the friend something positive that the visit has done for you. Such a simple comment as, "I feel better because of our visit," can be very important to the resident. This also contributes to the building of a mutually beneficial relationship.

Religion that is pure and undefiled before God and the Father is this: to visit orphans and widows in their affliction . . .

James 1:27

I never ask the wounded person how he feels; I myself become the wounded person.

Walt Whitman

5

Caring Through Visitation—II

Visiting the homebound, the hospitalized, or the nursing home resident is not uncommon among caring persons. However, there are other persons in need of the caring presence of friends. These persons are sometimes not accessible to the visitor, or the visitor is not comfortable in their presence. As a result, they have not enjoyed caring from the Christian community as often as have others. Such is true for persons in schools for the retarded, persons in prison, and persons hospitalized for mental illness.

Families with loved ones with such special needs are found in most congregations. These persons are not as widely known as others who live among us in the church fellowship. Even in our informed communities, some shame and fear surround retardation, the imprisoned, and those suffering mental illness. Caring persons hesitate to express their concern both for fear of being misunderstood and of feeling inadequate in the situation. Indeed, some families prefer that their loved one remain isolated from family friends. However, change is taking place in attitudes and practices. New care and treatment facilities encourage hope, and the heightened public consciousness surrounding individual human rights highlights unmet needs of many groups of persons, including these.

Caring Christian persons want to befriend such persons with special needs. This is difficult to do. One thing that the retarded, imprisoned, and mentally ill have in common is isolation. Unfortunately, this common element is a formidable one. Each of these groups of persons is isolated from social groups and cultural experiences which the rest of us take for granted. This isolation is a strong barrier, preventing the caring person from relating in a continuing way. Once the social and institutional barriers are bridged, the particular factors of each condition continue to make relating difficult. However, the barriers are not insurmountable. A person who cares can still go to a person in need, expressing love and hope. The effort can be made and friendships can be formed—love can be experienced.

Visiting the Retarded

Thousands of families throughout the world have retarded children. Three percent of all births in the United States are retarded babies.

"Mental retardation is a term used to describe conditions of impaired intellectual function. The impairment is such that the retarded person is handicapped in dealing with his or her environment."[31] The causing conditions usually appear before or shortly after birth. These causes include genetic, disease, and accident. The most widely known genetic cause is Down's syndrome or mongolism, when the fetus contains forty-seven chromosomes, rather than the normal forty-six. An example of retardation caused by disease is the result of the mother contracting rubella (three-day measles) during the first quarter of pregnancy. In an infant, high fever resulting from rubella can also

31. Robert Isaacson, *The Retarded Child, A Guide for Parents and Friends*. Argus Communications, 1974.

cause brain injury. (It must be noted that children have survived a fever of from 107 to 110 without resulting brain injury.)[32] Various accidents can cause brain injury to the infant or young child.

The development of new serums and other preventive means have reduced the incidence of retardation only somewhat. Also, prenatal testing for genetic disorders and other developmental malfunctioning have enabled physicians to discover when the fetus is not developing normally. However, the point has not been reached where many causes of retardation can be controlled.

Perhaps the greatest progress has been made in the public awareness of retardation and the families involved. Such families as the Kennedy family have highlighted the condition through their own experience. Recently, Mrs. Rose Kennedy wrote in *Family Weekly,* "It is hard to believe that only thirty years ago, when one of the founders of the Association for Retarded Citizens wanted to place a notice in her local newspaper asking other parents of special children to get in touch with her, the editor refused to let her sign her name or include her address. Mental retardation was considered a guilty secret to be wept over alone." Now the National Association for Retarded Citizens has more than 250,000 members, with some in every state. Many of these members are retarded themselves, and retarded youth and adults are workers in sheltered workshops and industry, where they earn all or part of their own livelihood.

Representing these gains is Public Law 94-142, passed by Congress in 1976, assuring that every retarded person will receive the benefits of public education suitable to the person's needs and abilities. Now, the states provide *schools* for the retarded, rather than homes or caretaker institutions. All but the most severely handicapped who live at the schools can learn, work, and play as their capacities allow.

---

32. *Ibid.*

Robert Meyers wrote a copyrighted article for the *Washington Post* in 1977 describing the wedding of his retarded, twenty-nine-year-old brother to a twenty-six-year-old, retarded woman. The groom was a busboy in a local restaurant (a suburban California community) and the bride was "studying to be a housewife." Both had IQs around seventy (mildly retarded). Mr. Meyers quotes authorities who agreed that fifteen years ago such a marriage could not have taken place. Such marriages are taking place now in many states.

Changing policies of families and institutions are resulting in the majority of retarded children being kept and cared for in the family, rather than being placed in institutions. The associations for mental health and mental retardation, with federal and state funding, have increased resources and facilities in local communities to make it possible for families to provide expert education and guidance for their retarded children. The special education resources of the public schools have made it possible for retarded children to live at home and to gain the benefits of education as their ability allows. The result has been that our communities and churches have retarded persons as citizens, many of whom can benefit from the same experiences as other persons.

The capacities and abilities of persons with below average intelligence range as widely as those with above average intelligence. The mildly retarded person, with an IQ in the 50-70 range, can learn to do many things, such as caring for personal needs, moving about in a familiar environment, learning routine work duties and carrying on a friendly conversation. By contrast, a severely retarded person with an IQ in the 20 to 35 range depends upon others for much care and supervision. There are various classifications used which are helpful in understanding the extent of variation in the abilities of retarded persons. The following table shows classifications commonly used:[33]

33. Isaacson, *The Retarded Child*, p. 95.

Degree of Retardation	Mental Age	IQ	Educational Classification
Mild	8-12	50-70	Educable
Moderate	5-8	35-50	Trainable
Severe	3-5	20-35	Trainable
Profound	0-3	0-20	Custodial

Current educational practice follows guidelines which place those who score from just under 80 IQ to just under 90 in the borderline category. Persons from just under 90 to 100 in IQ are considered as having no retardation. An IQ of 100 is the average or mid-point score for the entire population.

The most significant progress has been made in prevailing attitudes toward the retarded. Whereas thirty years ago families felt they had to isolate their child and not talk about retardation in the family, now families are able to take their retarded child with them many places. Churches have established special classes in religious education for children, youth, and adults. Several churches in a community will cooperate, with one age group meeting in one church, the others in other churches. One church, located near a sheltered workshop for retarded adults, sponsored a special class for the adults which numbered more than any other adult class in the church. The presence of these persons in the midst of the fellowship was a uniquely enriching experience for everyone in the church.

The need for special visitation of the retarded persons who live with their families is obviously not the same as for residents of schools for the retarded. Some of these have no close living relative; some have a parent who lives at a distance; some have been abandoned. There are some residents of the schools whose parents live nearby but seldom visit their child or relative. Some parents are unable to care for a retarded child.

The guidelines suggested here are for visitation of a resident in a state school for the retarded. They are given following an actual situation with the visitor describing the process in the first person.

Guidelines for Visiting a Retarded Person

1. Rev. and Mrs. Wilcox lived in my neighborhood and came to our church when they were in town on Sunday. Rev. Wilcox was retired but preached part-time for churches in the area when needed. Mrs. Wilcox's health required that they place their youngest daughter in the state school thirty-five miles away. I asked the Wilcoxes how they would feel about my visiting Jeanne at the school. They were pleased that I was interested in Jeanne and told me she would be delighted to see me.

2. I telephoned the Valley View State School for information about visiting. They were very helpful. I learned that they would like to have a note from one of Jeanne's parents about me so they could enter my name on the visitors' list. Friday was a regular visiting day with two periods available to me; from 1:00 to 2:15 P.M. or from 2:30 to 3:45 P.M. I told them I would be there on Friday ten days hence at 1:00 P.M.

3. I went directly to the administration building on the appointed day, and entered a visitors' reception area and lounge. It was crowded with persons waiting to see their friends and relatives. Since I arrived about five minutes early, it was only a few minutes until the receptionist called my name. Jeanne was waiting in another room next to the lounge area. We had the choice of going for a walk around the campus, visiting outdoors, or using the lounge area where there were soft drink and snack machines, TV, and table games available. Since it was such a nice day, we decided to walk. Jeanne wanted me to see the picnic area especially, and the chapel.

4. Jeanne's retardation was due to Down's Syn-

drome. She was short and stocky, with short arms and stubby fingers. Her tongue was large and her eyes were slanted (the source of the term "mongolism"). Jeanne had brown hair and eyes. She had been born late to her parents, her two older brothers having grown and married before her birth. She was then fifteen years old and had been in the state school for four years, classified as educably mentally retarded at the lower end of the mildly retarded range of IQ. I had learned this from her parents as we visited about my coming to see Jeanne. As we walked, Jeanne asked me questions about the town where her parents and I lived, and asked me if I knew one or two persons she had met on her brief visits home.

5. I soon discovered I needed to change my pattern of conversation. Jeanne would move suddenly from one subject to another. I did not need to ask many questions. She took me by the chapel where she went to church each Sunday and to choir practice. She was in the choir for the service designed for the more able students at the school. They learned the words to the hymns and enjoyed singing on Sunday. Jeanne also participated in a religious education class at the chapel one hour each week. Jeanne also took me to the store where she liked to spend her "tokens." These she earned by gaining points for personal grooming, the care of her living area, and carrying out her routine duties. Jeanne knew well the relative value for each colored token, exactly how much she had each day, and the value of the inexpensive camera for which she was saving.

6. Sometimes Jeanne did not pronounce words clearly, and I would have to ask her to repeat them. She also had a slight cold and would forget to wipe her nose promptly. I noticed these things, of course, but found that they really didn't interfere with our visit. At the picnic ground Jeanne met a friend visiting there with a parent, and Jeanne and her friend were proud to greet each other with their visitors. Jeanne smiled all the time and showed her pleasure in entertaining me.

7. As we returned from the picnic area, we met Chaplain "Van," as the students call him, walking with some visitors. Jeanne excitedly told him about me and talked so fast, the Chaplain had to interrupt. I was impressed with the way he talked with Jeanne. Without changing his voice or his manner from the way he spoke with me or the other visitors, he asked her to stop and start again, because he could not understand her. He communicated directly and precisely with her as if he were speaking to a younger person, but without talking "down" to her. It made me realize I had been using my voice very much like I do when talking to a small child. Jeanne is like a younger person in ability, but she is physically older and has more experience than the very young child. I learned a lot from listening to Chaplain Van talk with Jeanne.

8. Jeanne asked me the same questions several times during the visit. I answered them each time. She sometimes forgot, or she didn't listen to my answer. I just went on to something else. At times, Jeanne would be telling me about a friend and I could not follow everything she was saying, but it was all right. She just didn't fill in as many details as I am accustomed to, simply because she didn't know the details.

9. We walked back to the visitors' lounge because it was getting close to the end of our visiting period. At the door, Jeanne said, "I have to go now. Bye." And she walked away toward her residence hall. Didn't she like my visit? Didn't she want me to come back? Couldn't she have at least said, "Thank you for coming?" Of course she might, but she did not need to. It really was quite natural to end our visit that way.

10. I went to the desk and thanked the receptionist for the visit. She was a volunteer from town and checked me "out" on the visitors' list. She invited me to return on any visitors' day.

This is clearly the account of an "ideal" visit. Yet, it really happened. It may seem ideal because of many misconceptions about institutional care for the retarded in some state schools. On the other hand, not all visits go this smoothly, to be sure. Some of the residents are less able to respond than others, making it more awkward for the visitor and requiring more patience and understanding than this visit required.

You may be visiting a retarded person in the lower range of moderate retardation. If you have not met the person before, there may be awkward silences. Some simple activity is desirable, if the person you are visiting wishes it. A visitor might simply sit with the resident and watch a TV program, buy him or her a coke and candy bar. The visit might not take the full visiting period but be long enough for your concern and interest to be communicated.

Visiting the Imprisoned

Visiting persons in jails and prisons is considerably more limited than in other kinds of visitation. For the protection of the one imprisoned and for security, rules regulating visitation are more stringent. As a rule, visitation is usually limited to immediate relatives and officials, including legal counsel.

As is true for other kinds of public institutions, jails and prisons vary widely in their administration and in the rules that are followed. There are four general kinds of institutions for detention, with many variations under each category.

1. Jails and lockups. Most persons are acquainted with the existence of city and county jails. In most small communities, persons of legal age accused of breaking the law will be taken to the county jail. Here a person is held either temporarily until released on a bond or until arrangements are made for a hearing. City and county jails also house persons serving sentences, usually for not more than one year. The lockup serves the same purposes in the large cities, where each police precinct may have its own lockup to house offenders temporarily.

As a general rule, visitors are not allowed, except for official business, until some disposition of the case is made.

2. State prisons. Persons serving sentences for longer than one year are almost always taken to the state prison. In most states, provision is made for visitation, as well as for correspondence with inmates. The procedure varies from state to state, but all will have somewhat similar rules. In some state prisons, the inmate requests those names he or she wishes to have on a visitors' list and on a correspondence list. Persons not on the official list are not allowed visiting or correspondence privileges. Usually the inmate is given the right of refusal to see a visitor or to correspond with a given person.

3. Federal prisons. The federal government maintains a prison system to hold in detention persons who have broken federal laws. Over 250,000 persons are held in federal prisons each year. Gaining access to a person for visitation or correspondence sometimes is more difficult in maximum security prison units than in other prisons, but generally the procedures are similar.

4. Special detention institutions. These are for children and youth accused of crimes or delinquency. They are often called juvenile halls or juvenile homes. Youth are held in such homes because they have no home where necessary supervision and discipline is maintained. They are also held temporarily in such homes until time for a court hearing.

In recent years, both federal and state prison systems have instituted programs with varying degrees of freedom and rehabilitation for prisoners. There are minimum and maximum security prisons. Visitation in a minimum security prison which emphasizes rehabilitation allows for more personal contact with the inmates.

Frank had been arrested and found guilty on the second offense for stealing from an employer. The first offense happened when he was nineteen. Now he was twenty-one. Frank was a friendly, bright, handsome young man. He has always been able to convince persons of what he wanted them to believe about himself. He was put on probation after sentencing for the first offense. When the full impact of the sentence of three to five years in the state prison struck him, Frank fainted in the courtroom and had to be carried out to the first-aid room. Following release by the physician, Frank was placed in the county jail to await transportation to the state prison.

Frank's parents, active in church and community life, were under great stress. Frank had always been their favorite of three children. They had high hopes for his future. They were ashamed, hurt, and disconsolate. They were present in the courtroom when Frank fainted. When they got home, they called their pastor and another friend of long standing, whom they knew Frank liked very much. "Would you go to see Frank sometime before he is taken to the state prison?" they asked. Both the pastor and their friend agreed to go. They went on different days, and each was able to speak with Frank for ten minutes alone. The expressed concern of these two persons, probably more than that of the family, helped Frank to prepare himself for the days to come.

Frank was already showing attitudes and emotional responses often found in prison inmates, especially after long periods of incarceration. First, there was hostility—anger at anyone who would thwart Frank's desires. He believed that he should not be punished for taking someone else's money. The mixture of anger at his parents and his love for them left him feeling some guilt and shame in relationship to them. This same guilt and shame he did not associate with others. The experience of being caught and punished resulted in the beginnings of paranoia—the belief that persons were "after" him. He would not distinguish between those who legitimately would stop him from breaking the law and others' actions toward him.

At the age of twenty-one, Frank was showing signs of a character disorder in which he felt no conscience against committing a crime. The prison term probably will not help Frank to deal positively with all these feelings and attitudes—they may become worse. However, he was young enough that with early release for good behavior and some positive influences when he is released, he can yet overcome these serious problems.

Some or all of the attitudes and emotional responses are found in many imprisoned persons. The visitor should not be shocked or deterred seriously by them.

Guidelines for Visiting the Imprisoned

1. You will probably seek to visit a person whom you know or from a family you know. Visiting strangers in prison is usually not possible. Both denominational and interdenominational organizations sponsor chaplaincies for jails, and state and federal prisons have ministers on their staffs especially trained for prison chaplaincy. A congregation sometimes sponsors choir visits and prayer meetings in local jails. However, individual visitation with a person in prison requires different arrangements.

2. If you know the family members of the person you wish to visit, seek their support for your visit. Of course, there may be circumstances where this would not be possible or advisable, and you would proceed anyway. However, for continuing relationship with the person in prison, as well as his or her family, agreement for visitation or for correspondence is desirable.

3. Call or write the appropriate official in the prison or detention center for information to arrange a visit. In a state or federal prison, the office of the chaplain or the office of the assistant warden could supply the needed information. In a county jail, the sheriff's office will answer some requests.

4. In the event that your name must be placed on the inmates' visitor list, you can request the chaplain

or the assistant warden to ask the inmate to approve the addition of your name. If you know family members, of course, they can make the same request in their correspondence with the inmate.

5. Go to the jail or prison during the regular visiting hours, which in state and federal prisons are usually on Saturdays and Sundays. In state prisons, visiting hours may be set in time blocks, and the visitor must be present at the beginning of the block of time to gain entrance to the visitor building. Here, the visitor and the inmate can visit, separated by wire screen. Visits in city and county jails usually have to be for shorter periods of time, and without special visiting quarters, the visit must be done in the presence of a jailer. In minimum security institutions, more liberal conditions exist for visitation, allowing for more freedom of movement and privacy.

6. Your purpose in visiting the imprisoned is the same as visiting other persons with special needs: to establish a caring relationship with the person. This means that you express your interest and concern for the person as an individual and communicate your desire to be a friend.

7. In most instances, you will be visiting a person with quite different values and attitudes from your own. In addition, the pressures of incarceration, anger at authority, and resentment of "do-gooders" can make such a visit very trying. You have to *want* to visit a person in prison, and you must be able to accept the person you visit with all of his or her feelings and expressions.

8. Avoid arguments or attempting to *teach* the person in prison. You have *not* come to correct, reprove, or reform. You have come to attempt to show your concern—your caring for this person in this circumstance.

9. You may want or need to continue the relationship with correspondence and only intermittent visits. Subjects of interest to the person can be identified in this visit, making subsequent correspondence purposeful and more interesting.

10. Your religious experience and views may or may not be a welcome topic for discussion. As in other visits, take your lead from the person. If you ask, and the person does express interest, share the personal strength you find in your faith. It is always desirable to be prepared with a pocket Bible and perhaps a small devotional book which could be left as a gift. Encourage the person to share his or her own experience.

11. It is sometimes difficult to deal with requests which an inmate may make. It is not unusual for larger prisons to have printed visitation directions which give clear rules as to how to handle requests that some inmates make of visitors. For example, there may be a request that you contact a friend in order to convey some message. It is usually better to refer such a request to a family member or some other regular visitor or correspondent. Usually the message will be harmless and quite legitimate. It is not unknown for one in prison to attempt to use well-meaning persons to carry on illegitimate contacts with the outside.

12. Follow up your visit with a letter if that is possible. In some instances, further visits or correspondence will not develop. Where they can continue, your opportunity for positive influence may be significant.

Visiting the Mental Hospital Patient

As with the retarded, only a few years ago persons suffering from mental illnesses were feared, isolated, ignored, and degraded. Throughout history, persons with both physical and mental disorders were put to death out of ignorance and fear. Today in enlightened and affluent societies, persons with physical disorders are treated and cared for. We have not advanced so far in the treatment of mental illness. Treatment is still uneven and there is not the same tolerant attitude toward persons with mental illnesses. A person who has suffered a serious heart attack and recovered can be elected to high office; a person who has recovered from a "nervous breakdown" still cannot expect to survive politically.

Much progress has been made, however. Organizations and agencies, such as the National Association for Mental Health and the work of mental health and mental retardation agencies have helped educate the public. The necessity for change in attitude as well as for more and better treatment facilities is dictated by the scope of the problem. Over *half* of all our hospital beds are occupied by persons with mental illness. In addition, the Surgeon General of the United States estimates that in excess of 18,000,000 people are in serious need of expert help with their daily living. Various estimates are given to the percentage of persons who visit their physicians with physical ailments, also suffering from some form of mental illness. The estimates range from 25 to 50 percent.

Like physical illness, persons suffering from mental illness are often confronted with the necessity for hospitalization. Because of the stigma attached to mental hospitals, many persons understandably take every means to avoid them. In addition, the expense may be burdensome, especially when a person or a family seeks private medical care rather than to use publicly supported institutions. However, the very serious mental disorders require hospitalization because the person cannot remain safely at home. Not only is it unsafe and unwise for the patient, it may be damaging to others in the family.

While much is known about the nature of mental disorder, much remains to be learned. While research seeks to discover organic causes of mental illness, the results are often not definitive. Most persons who are mentally ill are diagnosed as having a *functional* disorder. Some functional disorders also have some organic factor involved. Ernest Bruder writes, "There is no sharp line of division between those who are 'mentally ill' and those who are 'mentally healthy'. . . . The present view is that mental health is a continuum from a condition of health or wholeness at one end of the scale through varying degrees of illness or disability to extreme 'sickness' at the other. The difference is of degree—quantitative rather than qualitative."[34]

No single cause of serious mental illness can be pinpointed. Mental illness is understood as a "set of complex responses to drastically changed conditions." In a *Clergyman's Guide to Recognizing Serious Mental Illness*,[35] Rev. Thomas W. Klink writes:

> The changes may occur in the person's body, in his mind, in his relationships with other people. The changes may appear to be very mild, such as the uncomplicated birth of a child or a simple change in job assignment. On the other hand, the changes may appear most severe: the sudden death of a spouse or the physical and social changes of aging. We know that there is considerable variance in the way people respond to extreme changes and to stressful situations.

The physician who is trained in psychiatry is the expert in mental illness. General hospitals often have special wards to which patients with mental illness are admitted for short-term treatment. Procedures vary from state to state and among hospitals within a state. Generally there is a time limit beyond which mental patients are not kept in a general hospital ward. Either the patient will be released, or sent to a state hospital or to a private treatment center.

Wherever possible, a person's agreement for hospitalization is obtained. A county judge has the power to commit a person to a mental hospital against the person's will, but most judges will not do so without careful investigation, including the judgment of one or possibly two psychiatrists. If a person needs to be hospitalized and refuses, the nearest relative can take the legal responsibility and ask the court to place the patient in the hospital.

---

34. *Ministering to Deeply Troubled People*. Fortress Press, 1967, p. 24.
35. Pamphlet prepared by The National Association for Mental Health, Inc., New York.

Every attempt is made to enable a person suffering mental illness to remain at home, obtaining out-patient treatment in a local hospital or with a psychiatrist in private practice. Hospitalization is generally reserved for more serious cases and for persons who cannot get adequate care elsewhere.

Guidelines for Visiting a Patient in a Mental Hospital

1. Since you will probably be visiting a relative of a friend or someone from your church or neighborhood, you will want to make this visit with the family's approval.

2. Like any hospital patient, the attending physician decides when the patient can see visitors. This is usually when the patient is in some phase of recovery. The family will usually know when the patient can see visitors, and whether it can be anyone beyond the family.

3. In the event you are allowed to visit, ask a relative who has visited the patient for suggestions as to the interests of the patient. It is not unusual for some particular subjects or events to be more disturbing to a patient than others. Some patients cannot discuss religion, with others it may be politics. With some, family concerns are not to be discussed with the patient.

4. Follow carefully the hospital rules for visitation, including time and place for the visit. Be sensitive to the well-being of the patient and time your visit accordingly.

5. Some patients will hardly speak at all; others may talk a great deal. As with other persons for whom you have interest and concern, follow the lead of the patient. Know subjects of interest to the patient and introduce these as you have opportunity. Pursue them only if the patient shows interest.

6. Use biblical material and prayer only if you are certain that it will help and not disturb the patient.

Use brief passages and brief prayers. Let the patient know of your continuing interest.

7. Reinforce hope and encouragement as expressed by the patient. Share your own positive response to the effort by the patient to get better. Express whatever positive outcomes you experience by making the visit.

8. When you return home, report your visit to the family along with your expressions of appreciation.

You may never be able to make such a visit because of a number of circumstances. In some instances, such a visit is not made because no one thinks of it or assumes it is not possible. Expressing your concern in itself may be a service to the family of the patient. Such concern is often finally communicated to the patient and hence has a healing effect as well.

We are afflicted in every way, but not crushed;
perplexed, but not driven to despair;
persecuted, but not forsaken;
struck down, but not destroyed;

Paul

Crises refine life. In them you discover what you are.

Allan Knight Chalmers

Your pain is the breaking of the shell that encloses your understanding.

Kahlil Gibran

6

Caring in Times of Crisis

Crises come to every person. They are a part of life. A crisis comes with terrible suddenness or it stealthily creeps up on us. As is true for all human experience, a crisis situation develops at a particular time and place, and the whole person is affected. A person experiencing a crisis responds physically and emotionally, and other persons become involved, directly or indirectly. Those who study the human response to crisis speak of it as "crisis management." We are learning to understand our responses enough that we can deal better with crises, with less negative and lasting results.

There are two kinds of crises: *natural* and *accidental*. Natural crises have to do with natural developments in a person's life cycle. As a person grows and develops, there is a whole series of crises, such as the young child leaving home to attend school for the first time, adolescent turmoil, preparation for marriage, or middle-aged trauma. Later, a person may find retirement from a rewarding vocation a true crisis experience.

Most of the time, when one speaks of facing a crisis, one thinks of accidental crisis: an incapacitating illness or accident, loss of a job, loss of one's home, or the death of a child. Such crises as these are brought on by an "abnormal" loss of that upon which one is dependent for a sense of welfare—of well-being.

The natural crises are "normal" in that they belong to a natural developmental process. Some persons seem to deal with such crises with little effort and pain while others show a great deal of anxiety and strain. Nevertheless, natural crises can be as traumatic as those of the accidental kind.

What is a crisis? The word "crisis" from the Greek *krisis* or *krinein* means "to separate." A crisis is a situation where a person's usual problem-solving abilities are insufficient to reduce the tension or difficulty. Gerald Caplan describes four phases in the development of a personal crisis:[36] (1) A problem causes tension which mobilizes the person's usual problem-solving responses; (2) Failure of the usual responses and the continuing tension result in inner disturbance such as guilt, disorganization, and ineffectiveness; (3) When this tension continues to mount, it stimulates stronger capacities within the person to meet the crisis; (4) If the tension continues unabated and the problem is not resolved, some major break in health can occur.

"Crisis-intervention" is spoken of by counselors and other mental health professionals as that process by which these phases are prevented from developing to the fourth or most destructive phase. Many of us may become involved in crisis-intervention when visiting friends after the death of a loved one, or visiting a person in the hospital following a severe heart attack. Persons are helped to manage both natural and accidental crises in their lives by the caring relationship of others.

Jerry and Joy Michaels and their three-year-old daughter had just moved into their own home. They had lived in a small apartment for the first years of their marriage and both had worked in order to save for the down payment. At work, Joy received a call from the hospital telling her that Jerry had been injured. Joy went at once and found that Jerry had suffered a fall resulting in serious injuries to one arm and

36. *Principles of Preventive Psychiatry*. Basic Books, Inc., 1964.

to both legs. He would recover, but the prognosis was uncertain as to recovery of the full use of both legs.

As the days passed and the injuries began to heal, Jerry became depressed because he was sure he would not be able to return to work. This would mean that they would have to sell the house and move in with his parents. Joy didn't see the situation that way. The physicians believed that with physical therapy, Jerry could recover the use of his legs, and Joy had the assurance of the company that time would be allowed for Jerry's recovery. She believed they could count on emergency help from parents and friends.

The four major phases in the development of a crisis are illustrated by the experience of Jerry and Joy. The first is the external cause or event. In this case, the accident itself was the external event. The next step is the person's appraisal of the situation. Jerry's appraisal was more pessimistic than was Joy's. (They could have been reversed.) The third phase is how the person can marshal personal resources to deal with the situation as he or she perceives it. Fourth, the person is in the crisis itself, responding internally to the external situation.

Under the stress of sudden external change, a person is stunned and momentarily unable to bring coping strengths to bear upon the situation. Joy's appraisal was more objective than was Jerry's, and it took some time for him to appraise it in a more hopeful way. Joy's appraisal and strength enabled Jerry to have a glimmer of hope and to begin to bring his own internal strength to bear upon the situation. He began to regain his confidence, and as his body healed, so did his self-confidence in picking up where he had suddenly been interrupted in his work and family life.

Three other crisis-producing situations will be discussed here because of their universal occurrences. Caring persons can become significant resources for persons experiencing these crises. The first is crisis brought on by the death of a loved one, the second is crisis brought on by marital separation and/or divorce, and the third is crisis brought on by retirement from work. Notice that in each of these crises, a person loses *something* or *someone* important. Grief is acute sorrow. We grieve over the loss of someone or something of meaning and significance to us. In loving relationships, coming together brings fulfillment and joy, while moving apart brings loneliness and sorrow. All of us experience separation from loved ones, fortunately in most instances, for short periods of time. Your separation from your mother at birth was your first traumatic separation. Birth results in all the physical and emotional outcomes of human separation. As mentioned earlier, the infant requires at least a year to adapt to that separation, growing into a separately functioning individual.

As the infant grows through childhood and youth into adulthood, many other important separations take place. The kindergartner is separated from mother and home. The high school graduate is separated from family by leaving to go to college, or into the military service, or to work. The young adult leaves one family to form another in marriage. So the cycle begins afresh, the interweaving of gaining and losing life-giving human relationships.

Loss and grief, then, are a part of all three of these crisis experiences—the death of a loved one, marital separation and/or divorce, the loss of meaningful work. Grief is the natural human response to significant loss. It is healthy for a person to experience and to express feelings of grief. Yet, out of the lack of information and understanding, some persons attempt to suppress their grief. Some believe this is necessary to be "strong" or that the expression of grief will be understood by others as a lack of Christian faith.

Visiting the Bereaved

A young minister just beginning seminary study became confused between theological dimensions of faith and expressions of grief by his parishioners at funerals. Being emotionally uninvolved in their loss, he sought through preaching to convince them of the need to be "joyful" at the death of a loved one, for the deceased now had come into the ultimate fulfillment of life. It was as he began to experience significant loss himself that he knew the two were not mutually exclusive—that Christian hope and loss and grief are experienced together.

Following a catastrophic fire in Boston many years ago in which hundreds of persons died suddenly, Dr. Erich Lindemann, a professor of psychiatry at Harvard, conducted a study of the grief processes of the survivors. The study clearly delineated the kind of "work" a person has to do in order to recover from a significant loss. This "grief work" centers largely around five things which Dr. Lindemann observed.

1. Acute grief results in physical distress. The body has not been injured, but because we are *whole* persons, shock and distress in one area affects the other areas as well. The deep emotional response to the loss leaves mental and physical effects. Some common physical distress includes loss of appetite, listlessness, weariness, and nausea. All persons will not experience exactly the same kinds of physical distress, of course. Some will become physically ill and not be able to take nourishment at all. Others will eat normally but experience other physical symptoms, including pain in various parts of the body.

2. Acute grief produces a preoccupation with the image of the deceased. The accustomed physical presence of the loved one lingers in the life of the grieving person. This can be very strong at first and takes varying amounts of time to gradually lessen and to disappear.

3. Acute grief includes guilt feelings. Death, even when anticipated, *always* comes before we are prepared. Human relationships, even the most loving, are still human and thus incomplete. We feel guilty for words said or not said, for deeds done or left undone, for not being what we always thought we should be to the loved one. "If I had just gotten here on time." "If

we just hadn't quarrelled two weeks ago—I never said I was sorry!" These and other such expressions reveal the guilt which must be "worked through" in the grief process.

4. Acute grief includes hostile reactions. Since anger is such an important part of our normal emotional life, anger can be expected to become a part of our grief work. Unresolved anger at the loved one may be repressed since one cannot be angry at a loved one who is dead. This is unacceptable to oneself, and one imagines it would be unacceptable to others. It is not unusual for a young child to become angry at a parent who dies and leaves him "all alone." Not finding opportunity to express the anger and to have it accepted, the child often finds no way to become aware of it by expressing it, until in the adult years when some other crisis brings the anger to the surface.

5. Acute grief brings the loss of patterns of conduct. The loss is so disruptive of one's whole accustomed patterns of thinking and acting that it temporarily results in disorganization. One young man whose mother had died noticed a carload of laughing teenagers driving by and said, "How can anybody be happy today?" There comes a sense of physical detachment as well as mental detachment leaving a grieving person bewildered. The social custom of not returning to work for a week or so following the death of a loved one has its beginning in the recognition of this change. To be sure this is more acute for some persons than for others.

While these five components of grief were identified by Lindemann in persons grieving over the death of loved ones, the same responses are experienced after any significant loss. They can be as real for a newly divorced person and for a person in the first days of retirement. Grief follows the loss of something or someone that is important to us.

Anticipatory Grief

Grief is also expressed in anticipation of a loss. All the phases of grief are expressed in advance, to "prepare" a person for the impact of the actual death or loss. Such was true for Joan, anticipating the death of her mother. Her mother was in her eighties, paralyzed and in a coma for three weeks, and Joan found herself going through the grief process. She knew that death was inevitable and felt guilty for grieving as long as her mother held on to life. Yet, it seemed natural to prepare for the finality of death.

The work of Dr. Elizabeth Kubler-Ross with terminally ill patients, in which she identified five stages through which dying patients moved, has become familiar to many persons.[37] One friend or family member may not identify all of these clearly in experiencing the death of a loved one. However, each of these will probably be manifested in feelings and responses in some ways.

1. Denial or disbelief. In anticipating one's own death or that of a loved one, the shock of the first realization seems to cause one to "hold back" from what is happening. The natural outcome is to feel alone and to withhold feelings.

2. Anger. Misfortune never appears to be just. "Why should this happen to us?" We need to find out *why*. God is often held responsible, either in resigned acceptance or with hostility. The *resigned* acceptance often is made out of the fear of openly blaming God, but the underlying anger may be just as real as openly expressed hostility.

3. Bargaining. Following the first shock waves and the feelings of anger, there is often some kind of bargaining, either with God through prayer, or with physicians, or between the patient and a survivor. This is not seen as something to be avoided but to be understood. The careful examination of the past and the present, with projection into the future, is natural. Many alternative ways of thinking and dealing with this death are examined, with the unrealistic ways gradually being eliminated. Thus is enhanced the

---

37. *On Death and Dying*. Macmillan Co., 1969.

possibility of fully accepting those that are possible and real.

4. Despair. The natural fourth stage is despair, the deep mourning of inevitable loss, with accompanying pain, family disorder, possible financial strain, and relational disruption. The physical and emotional signs of depression are present: lack of appetite, listlessness, withdrawal, general inability to function normally.

5. Acceptance. The final stage, which most grieving persons are naturally able to come to, is acceptance of the loss. This is not the same as resignation. To become resigned is to live with something against one's will or inner being. Acceptance is the incorporation of the reality into one's being, allowing a return to a full and balanced experience of life.

These same five phases of the grief process can be seen in the anticipation of the death of a marriage, or in the loss of meaningful work or other relationships. The sense of *loss* is the catalyst to grieving. One example not as often identified is the high percentage of our population grieving daily as they move to a distant place to build relationships all over again. Some are able to resolve it in a short time, given off-setting joys and satisfactions by the move, while others may take many months to find the final stage of acceptance.

It is at the time of significant loss that grieving persons may be strengthened by the understanding visit of a caring friend. Since each person and situation is unique, careful preparation and judgment is imperative. We go to visit only after reassurance that we are welcome and the time is right. The caring presence and loving expression are bridges for the grieving person trying to cross the chasm of despair.

Guidelines for Visiting the Bereaved (Death)

1. Prepare for the visit. Ask your pastor for necessary information, such as, when and where is the

funeral, what funeral home is handling the funeral, when will the family be at home receiving visitors.

2. Decide when to visit. In many instances, families appreciate the presence of friends at the funeral home an evening or two prior to the funeral, as well as visits in the home. Following the custom of your community, the needs of the family, and your relationship with them, decide what conditions you prefer in making your visit. Usually a visit in the home affords a more personal visit.

3. Visit in the home at appropriate hours. Avoid visiting too early in the day or at mealtimes. Do not expect to stay at length. Take your clue from the family members as to the length of the visit.

4. Express your love and concern. Speak to your grieving friend(s) as soon as possible upon arrival. Make your expression clearly and unhurriedly, but briefly. Avoid "teaching" statements such as, "I'm sure God knows best," or "We are not given to understand." Rather, share your own positive feelings of grief and loss, as well as how you are exercising your faith. (Such a statement might be something like, "My heart aches because I have lost a dear friend. I am praying that God's love is with you, especially now. I love you.")

5. Be alert to a task you can accomplish or an errand you can run. You don't always need to *ask* to be of service. Sometimes the question is asked and taken as a social custom, rather than in an expectation of being carried out. If you ask, it might be appropriate anytime during the visit.

6. Be prepared to listen. This is especially important when you are the only visitor present. It is often helpful to speak of the deceased in a warm and personal way. The response your friend makes may be important for his or her expression of grief.

7. Be prepared to offer your comforting presence. You may become a vital catalyst for grief expression. It is imperative that you can accept crying without threat or embarrassment. It is not inappropriate for you to share in such open expression, remembering you

are there as a source of strength and comfort as well. You will not be surprised if there are expressions of anger and/or guilt as your grieving friend struggles toward acceptance of the loved one's death.

8. Offer to share in reading of scripture and prayer. Many grieving persons ask the visitor to choose a passage, while some ask for a favorite passage that comes to mind. Have one or two comforting passages marked in your pocket Bible and turn to them easily and quickly. Let your prayer be personal and simple, including expressions of gratitude for aspects of life and death, of love among persons, and including petition for God's continuing healing presence. Other expressions centering in themes of hope, growth, forgiveness, and grace may be especially strengthening for your friend.

9. As you leave, you may find this the time to offer your assistance, such as with transportation, child care, meal preparation, communication, or other arrangements. If you are given opportunity to help, be prepared to do so as quickly as indicated by the situation.

10. Express your availability at any time of need. This may be more important for your grieving friend a week after the funeral than it is now. Many persons may share their love at this time of special need, not as many are able to follow through in days to come.

11. Convey any growth and understanding you may have gained through sharing loss and grief with your friend. This too may come some time later.

Many important and significant gifts help to convey our feelings of compassion and loss with others. Not only is there a sharing of food around a table of love, but there are small, personal gifts that sometimes convey better than words how we share in time of crisis. Your own experience will help you to make such a selection. Its presentation is made privately and quietly, in harmony with the genuineness of your love.

Visiting the Separated and Divorced

When we remember that the incidence of divorce continues to rise inexorably toward the 50 percent figure, we realize how many persons there are about us who experience the pain of separation. For many persons, it is difficult to express concern when a couple separates. There are several reasons: we wish to respect the couple's privacy; we are sensitive to the danger of taking "sides" in a marital dispute; we are reluctant to be seen as offering "help" when we know we probably cannot. As a natural consequence, we say nothing about a separation or divorce, other than to offer our sympathy when the matter has become "public." Often, that follows the notice of "divorces asked" in the local newspaper. For the persons suffering marital discord, it is natural to want privacy, for reason of guilt and/or shame and sometimes in the hope that the relationship can be healed. Needing the comfort and support of friends but feeling the need to keep silent, they suffer alone.

Separation from the person you once loved and gave yourself to brings a full range of emotions. Three which are almost universally experienced are (1) a sense of failure, (2) guilt, and (3) loss.

1. A sense of failure. Most marriages begin with the expression of love, hopeful anticipation for the future, and some sense of achievement. "I have found the person I was looking for," or "Now I can have the family I always dreamed of" express rather common feelings. When a couple separates, and this love, hope, and sense of achievement disappears, often in the midst of charges and recriminations, a sense of failure is a natural outcome. Sometimes, it is projected to the partner in an effort to avoid accepting *any* failure consciously. Yet it is there in most instances. This sense of failure may be greatly enlarged when children are present at the time of separation. Most parents in our culture want to be good parents. Separation and divorce are seen generally as detrimental to developing children. As each person in a dissolved marriage

redoubles efforts to be a good parent, the result is often experienced by the child ambiguously, at best. As the parent perceives this response from children, the sense of failure increases.

A natural result of a sense of failure is a lowered self-esteem. The sense of failure through divorce can deliver a severe blow to some persons' self-esteem. Feeling both a failure and a person of questionable worth, such a person becomes vulnerable to breakdown. In any case, the negative self-image becomes very difficult to overcome. Emotionally vulnerable persons can become victims of others with whom they normally would not develop significant relationships. Some second marriages, which also fail, take place in such an emotionally disturbed time.

2. Feelings of guilt. Most of us feel some guilt when we fail, or believe we have. This is particularly true in human relationships. Taking the marriage vows becomes a sacred trust to many persons, and those vows are broken only with accompanying guilt. Real guilt is finally resolved only when a person seeks and gains a sense of forgiveness. Whose forgiveness can a divorced person seek? The conditions of the breakdown of relationship often preclude the gaining, if not the asking, of forgiveness. Thus, the guilt is carried by the person until absolution is offered and accepted through religious ritual or through successful therapy.

3. Sense of loss. It is ironic that a ruptured love relationship resulting in separation and divorce can leave a person feeling loss. It is true that some persons find a sense of release and joy, with no apparent loss. Yet, few persons do not feel some loss, even though it may be limited to the loss of familiar living patterns. Loneliness is a predominant outcome of such loss. Those suffering extreme loss will go through the same grief reaction as if suffering loss by death.

No matter how difficult a relationship has been, loneliness often follows separation. New relationships and continuing meaningful activity are the necessary antidotes to debilitating loneliness.

Fred, a minister, and Marian had been married for twelve years when she filed for divorce. Marian was angry at Fred, and had been for some time. Fred wanted custody of the boys, eleven and nine. Feeling inadequate as a mother, a failure as a minister's wife, and wanting a different life-style, she agreed to give up her children. The sense of failure, the lowered self-esteem, and the accompanying guilt, pushed her into a depression. Seeking counseling, Marian gradually recovered and ultimately married a second time, happily.

During her separation and divorce, Marian experienced loneliness she had never known before. Following her decision to divorce Fred, she moved to another community and, with counseling, sought to renew old friendships and to create new ones. Referring to those difficult days, Marian told her counselor, "Two caring friends helped me, mainly at the times of deepest loneliness."

Guidelines for Visiting the Separated and Divorced

1. Telephone your friend or acquaintance and inquire when you might come for a brief visit. With established friends, extending an invitation to join you for church, lunch, or some entertainment is appropriate. However, for those you may not know, a visit may be best. Mention that you are aware of the person's recent separation or divorce and want to express your friendship.

2. Upon arrival, tell your purpose in coming, in your own words. Your motivation is to establish or develop a friendly relationship, not to seek information.

3. As conversation develops, try to follow and not lead. However, be active so that conversation can progress in a lively way.

4. In the event your friend speaks of the separation or divorce, listen with the same interest and skill as in the other situations discussed earlier.

5. If asked by your friend to agree or to confirm judgments in regard to the separation, reply that you could not say, but you want to understand your friend's situation. Your visit may enable the person to verbalize feelings or to weigh alternatives for a decision, although this would be unlikely unless a relationship has been established.

6. Be prepared to offer referral help if your friend expresses need and desire for counsel. Avoid speculation concerning legal matters. Your encouragement toward referral is usually most effective following your friend's expression of need.

7. If you don't know about the person's church relationship, inquire. If your friend is open, invite him or her to your church for worship or an activity with you (and your family) at a specified time.

8. Make your judgment as to the person's receptivity to prayer. Your expression of concern, that your prayers for others will include him or her today and tomorrow, may meet the need most effectively.

9. Make the length of the visit fit the situation. Often, a visit of twenty to thirty minutes is adequate. However, if the relationship develops quickly, more time may be necessary.

10. Upon leaving, make firm the arrangements for the later appointment.

Remember that some recently separated or divorced persons may not be receptive to a visit when others will. The expression of caring amidst respect for the person and his or her own privacy is the only goal. This may be accomplished by a brief telephone conversation when a visit is not possible. The reaching out to lonely and troubled persons is paramount—all else takes its meaning and direction from the caring expression.

Visiting the Retired

Retirement is a major turning point in adult life. Since it marks the transition from middle life to old age, retirement is a major personal and social event. The number of retired persons in our communities is increasing rapidly. In 1940 there were 9 million retired persons in the United States, in 1970 there were 20.2 million and in 2000, there will be 29 million.[38] As life spans lengthen, more and more persons are living to retirement age and considerably beyond.

The Meaning of Work

Sidney Jourard points out that "One can work to earn a livelihood, to avoid boredom in life, or to fulfill the meaning of one's life."[39] For many persons in our culture, the core of life's meaning is found in one's work. In part, this seems to be related to our achievement-oriented society and the Christian work ethic. Worthy persons are seen as those who work, who produce, and "make a contribution." A person gains self-esteem from such achievement through work, for it uplifts one in the eyes of others. For example, its import is seen in the use of the question, "What do you do?" as well as "What is your name?" in identifying ourselves with one another. For many persons, identification with one's work becomes the single most important identification made in life, sometimes beyond one's own closest relatives.

For these reasons and others, meaningful work is seen as essential for healthy personality. Meaningful work covers a wide territory: it may be for remuneration or not. What is important is that each person finds some fulfillment in the work that is done so that some pride is felt in doing it. Thus, there is little mystery surrounding the importance of a person's retirement from meaningful work.

The Meaning of Retirement

Douglas C. Kimmel identifies three distinct ele-

38. Douglas C. Kimmel, *Adulthood and Aging*. John Wiley and Sons, 1974, p. 256.
39. *Healthy Personality*. Macmillan Publishing Co., 1974.

ments in retirement: an *event*, a *status*, and a *process*.[40] These elements are helpful in clarifying the meaning of retirement.

1. Retirement as an event. Until recently, the Social Security law dictated the time of retirement for vast numbers of persons. This has been operant since the 1930s until 1978 legislation changed the mandatory age for retirement for many. As an event, retirement marks the end of work and the beginning of leisure. It is interesting to note that while companies and institutions may have a ceremony and present the employee of twenty, thirty, or forty years with a watch or a certificate, there is little other social recognition of the event in a person's life. There are exceptions, of course, but for the vast majority of persons, this important turning point in life is not marked by ceremony. Other significant events in the life span are more socially recognized, such as graduation from college, marriage, the birth of a baby, a particular outcome of the productivity of work. By comparison, the ceremony surrounding the *event* of retirement is often lacking.

The elected president of a national professional organization came to the last day of office (after a tenure of two years) and remarked, "I just now realize I need something to help me let go." There had been no public recognition of his leaving office, despite the fact he was loved and valued by the organization. This illustrates how such a need may be compounded many times over when a person leaves work to which he or she has given himself or herself at length.

2. Retirement as a status. A number of important changes come about upon retirement. They involve a whole new social position, with different roles and expectations from those which a person has been living with for many years. Three of the most important have to do with reduced income, increased leisure time, and family readustment. There are both positive and negative aspects to each of these. While a reduced

40. *Adulthood and Aging*. p. 255.

income is largely negative, the increase of leisure time is usually seen by the person and by society as a positive factor in an individual's status. One of the most poignant TV advertisements by an insurance company shows the retired man gazing longingly at a ship departing from port and commenting something like this, "I have always wanted to take a trip on one of these, but now that I have time to do it, I don't have the money."

Due to difference in age at marriage, and the difference between men and women in life expectancy (men, 68; women, 76), as well as differences in work, retirement almost always results in a readjustment of the marriage relationship. For those spouses left alone through death, readjustment may be necessary in relation to other family members, whether in the same household or not. One man, living alone and recently retired, spoke of his activity. "I read a little, and walk a mile and half a day. I walk down to my daughter's house two or three times a week and visit with the family." Whereas before he seldom spent time in his daughter's house, now all at once it is increased dramatically. Both he and his daughter's family have adjustments to make in the relationship.

3. Retirement as a process. Increasingly, persons are being helped to *plan* for retirement. This change in the public view from that of ignoring it until it arrives, to recognizing the need to prepare and to do so positively, is an important shift. As is true for all life's important transitions, the more it can be engaged as a *process* as well as an *event,* the easier the transition.

Biological factors make it a process. Not all retire because of poor health, but the estimate is that about one-half currently retiring, do so because of poor health. Whether retirement is forced or voluntary affects the process of retirement. Forced retirement, especially when a person continues in good health and productivity, can become a serious barrier for a person to overcome.

A major study of retirement done at Cornell University in 1971 brought reassuring results. Over 1,486 men and 483 women nearing retirement age in the 1950s were studied in depth over a period of time.[41] It was found, for example, that there were far fewer negative outcomes generally associated with retirement than most persons assume. The person's prior *attitudes* about retirement emerged as more critical than whether retirement was voluntary or forced. These persons adapted to change in role and status in much the same ways as they had adapted to critical changes in earlier experiences.

Retirement can be a positive and meaningful transition in the lives of persons, another doorway to continuing growth and development. Thp rocess is important and positive attitudes vital.

Guidelines for Visiting the Retired

1. If possible, visit *newly* retired persons, as they are in the midst of important adaptations to retirement.
2. Seek to discover the state of health of the retired person before you go. The visit will require different considerations if the retired person is ill and/or bedfast.
3. Assuming the full health of the retired person, prepare to make your visit as with any friend. The person's greatest need may well be the continued daily contact with persons outside the home.
4. In addition to the visit, and in determining the interests and activities of the person, take the initiative in joining your friend in some activity. For example, the golfer usually looks for another likely partner.
5. In some instances, you may find a person struggling with relational tensions in the home, with new roles and responsibilities to adjust to. If so, a prolonged visit may be out of place.

---

41. *Adulthood and Aging*. p. 258.

6. In natural ways, without manufacturing them, look for common interests and activities in which you can offer companionship or encouragement. The church and full participation in its activities is a good example. Follow up when an opportunity comes by any appropriate means.

7. Remember that adjustment to retirement may include the grief reaction following this significant loss. Be alert to the feelings and other signals of discouragement and depression.

As time passes in retirement, with loss of family and accustomed friendly encounters, loneliness becomes a constant companion to many persons. The caring visits can break the lonely stretches and provide the needed human encounter. In the quality of the caring relationship resides the saving power of love. Its expression among the retired of our communities will enrich all who engage in it.

And he who searches the hearts of men knows what is the mind of the Spirit, because the Spirit intercedes for the saints according to the will of God.

Roman 8:27

Join the great company of those who make the barren places of life fruitful with kindness. Carry a vision of heaven in your heart, and make the world correspond to that vision.

Helen Keller

7

Sustained in Caring

Christian caring is sustained by God's love and our response to that love. Caring acts carried out over time require both commitment and self-discipline. What are the sources in sustaining caring activity? As in all Christian history, our strength and resolve for service are drawn from worship in the faith community and from personal devotional living.

Sustained in Caring Through Worship

The public worship of God rests at the core of sustaining caring relationships. Here, the meaning of our existence and the direction for activity are given. Removed from the act of public worship, we lose hope for the continuance of life itself. What happens to us in the act of worship? We encounter the living God. What is the shape of that encounter and what does it mean for sustaining us as caring persons?

A. God, once again, becomes the focus for our lives. In the daily round, focus diffuses, fades in and out. We are diverted and lose our concentration within the complex activity of living. New foci appear, seductively and suddenly. They are enticing and strong: the lure of property and power; the excitement of sexual encounter; the satisfactions of leisure pursuits;

the heady well-being of popular acclaim; the languid half-light of laziness; the self-destructiveness of dependency; the death of isolation. Then, called back for "centering in," we go to worship. God remains at the center of life and we are confronted with that reality above all others. Our response is adoration. God *is* great. God *is* good. Holy *is* his name. We recover our balance and our sense of who we are. Created lovingly by God and nurtured into caring persons, we are renewed by that love.

This refocusing is essential for sustaining caring relationships. We care because we are cared for. But only as we tend to the reordering of our priorities, can we maintain our identity as caring persons.

B. In the worship encounter, we are confronted anew with the imperative to surrender ourselves. Much of our energy is expended in attacking, not surrendering. Life seems to call for advancing, charging forward. History teaches us that individuals as well as nations have to discover the secret of when to attack and when to surrender. Statesmen negotiate, parliaments and legislatures debate, armies train—all within an ebb and flow of attacking and retreating.

All about us are admonitions to be more forceful, to learn how to become "assertive." Some of us should grow in self-assertion. However, the pressures make it difficult to find time and place for peaceful and health-giving surrender. The key, of course, is to whom do we surrender and when. Within Christian worship, we surrender ourselves to God and to his purposes. The means is confession. Many life experiences are humbling and discouraging. However, it is not until the Christian penitent is engaged in such activity as prayer, or in partaking of bread and wine at the Lord's Table, that confession can bring him or her to the threshold of surrender. Only as we give up, can we gain. And only as it follows the refocusing of ourselves and our goals upon God does surrender take on positive force for growth and change.

Surrendering ourselves in confessional posture sustains us in our caring relationships. Error and pride are kept within manageable boundaries. Without this worship discipline our sense of service can deteriorate into self-grandeur. Through confession and surrender to God, we are able to continue to know our human imperfection, allowing us to accept the imperfections of others.

C. In the worship of God, in company with our fellows, we regain our childhood eagerness for life. If routine in our lives provides order and security, it can also deaden the sensitivity to life's blessings. When activity becomes so complex and persistent that even momentary thoughts of gratitude are crowded out, caring suffocates. Caring is reborn in worshipful thanksgiving. When one loses sight of the grace of God, caring withers for lack of nourishment.

Every human relationship is enriched when the persons involved experience gratitude—for the gift of life, for the joy of love, for the satisfaction of giving. It is gratitude, even in the face of overwhelming adversity, that saves us from utter despair. When all else is taken away, there remains that miraculous gift of life itself. The caring Christian's hope is fixed upon the openness of that life. In God's time and purpose, human death cannot limit its nature or boundaries.

D. In worship, we are enabled to claim God's forgiveness. It "helps" to praise God, to surrender to him in confession, to find expression for gratitude—but to claim the forgiveness of God becomes mandatory to be sustained in caring. It is difficult for the caring Christian to worship and to partake of the Lord's Supper and *not* lay hold of God's forgiveness.

Our relationships with others, if they are healing in their nature, embody forgiving love. The small amount within us needs tender nurturing—in the worship of God. We go to worship, not to get or to give—but to *be*. We are there as God's own. He has known it all along—we forget it daily. We come away refreshed in that rediscovery and renewed as caring Christians.

Sustained in Caring Through Personal Devotional Life

The word "devotional," means "with ardent attachment or affection, with loyalty." We are sustained in caring through loyalty to personal values, thoughts, and practices. The public worship of God provides us with the center. Moving out from the center, we form concentric circles of thought and practice which provide further means of sustaining caring.

A. We are sustained in our caring through thought and prayer. Do you ever ask yourself, "What do I think about all day long?" We would be astounded to learn how many different thoughts flash through our minds in a minute's time, not to mention within a whole day. The popularity of myriad techniques for meditation described in paperback books attest to the wide interest in such ordering of thought.

Meditation—the careful disciplining of thought—has always been a part of the Christian experience. Disciplined thought, directed to God, we know as prayer. Through meditation and prayer, we are reminded that many of our thoughts can be controlled, that they are within the purview of our wills and our desires. There are the exceptions—in time of stress through illness, injury, loss, and grief. But for much of life's experience, we control thought.

The caring Christian recognizes the need for such discipline. There is a time during each day when we are renewed through personal prayer and reflection upon the meaning of life. We can lay hold of devotional resources which have become classic in Christian literature as well as the Bible itself for guidance and direction.

B. We are sustained through reading and study. As caring persons devoting ourselves to forming and maintaining positive relationships, we confront new experiences and new questions. A visit to the sick room of a terminally ill friend, talking with a friend whose child has run away from home, sitting with a friend whose teenage son has just died from an overdose of drugs—all such experiences push us to read and study.

C. We are sustained in caring through the way we see life. Drawing upon the resources of thought, reflection and prayer, reading and study, and through worship, we maintain a singular vision of life. It is sacred; it is growing and developing; it is eternal. Jesus spoke of our having eyes to see and ears to hear. They are the windows and the receivers bringing us constant, pulsating messages of life in stereo.

As we see, hear, and respond to our neighbors, who stand with us before a living God, we find our Christian calling—to love God and neighbor.